Coping with Stress
for Academic Success:
24 Strategies to Get the Most Out of Your
Educational Experience

Carlton H. Oler, Ph.D., BCPCC

DEDICATION

This book is dedicated to all my students—past, present, and future—who long for their educational experience to be less stressful and more fulfilling.

CONTENTS

ACKNOWLEDGMENTS

First and foremost, I must thank God the Father, God the Son, and God the Holy Spirit for privileging and enabling me to complete this book—He continues to bless despite my undeservedness. I must thank Gene Ahwah Oler, Ph.D., MSW for her support and valuable feedback, and Pastor Pierre F. Steenberg, Ph.D., D.Min. for his incredibly generous help. I must also thank Ms. Amy Chirman, M.L.S. and Mr. Clifford R. Goldstein, M.A. for their editing expertise. Last, but not least, I must thank my students—from the academically lax to academically perfectionistic—for providing a window into their respective worlds.

INTRODUCTION

Many students stress out about school. For many, "stress" is their middle name. Much of this stress is self-inflicted (students' bring it on themselves), but some is inherent to the academic arena itself. Lack of personal insight and awareness of simple strategies can keep students captive to poor self-discipline, disorganization, procrastination, poor academic performance, low self-worth, chronic relationship problems, addictions, poor sleep, poor physical health, (the list goes on) and destined for a potential-inhibiting and dissatisfying academic experience. Though students range from the academically lax to the academically perfectionistic, all want good grades. Students along this continuum often encounter stress in multiple areas, which can negatively affect their academic success.

The purpose of this book is to provide students with insights and strategies to reduce the stress in several student-relevant areas. These insights and strategies have been effective in reducing or eliminating stress for many students. Many have stated that these concepts have prevented the stress that would have, otherwise, hurt their educational experience. Both students and non-students have found that these counsels apply to *life success* in general.

Though this book is primarily geared for students, those who work with students (such as educators and academic and personal counselors) will find it useful in appreciating the multiple stresses students contend with and as a means to provide help. Parents of students, through reading this book, will gain greater insight into the challenges students face, and be better able to support them to get the most out of their educational investment.

In this book I define "stress" as any thought, feeling, ignorance (misinformation or lack of information), or behavior relative to the self, a situation, or a relationship that *adversely impacts* the self, a situation, or a relationship. I define "academic success" as enjoying the educational process and learning something meaningful or useful, whether or not a desirable grade is achieved.

Coping with stress is a formidable task. However, with Holy Spirit inspired self-discipline—that is, by doing what you must do, whether you feel like it or not, *because it needs to be done*— stress can be conquered.

CHAPTER 1

Develop a Self-Change Plan

There's a saying: "Those who fail to plan, plan to fail." It's also true that plans not written down are often soon forgotten and never achieved. Coping with stress for academic success is achieved by practicing intentional or planned behavior. If you want to succeed here, your behavior will have to change.

What better way to shift behavior into academic success mode than to develop a self-change plan? However, before you develop this plan, it's essential to earnestly seek the Lord's will in prayer. He will tailor your plans so that you glorify Him, and experience abundant personal fulfillment.

A self-change plan involves writing down (1) the challenges or problems you're already aware of or identify from reading this book, (2) the goals for the challenges or problems you've identified, and (3) your plan (the behaviors you'll perform) to achieve the goals for your challenges or problems. The plan must be realistic *and* specific, making it easy to identify at any time what you're working on and the degree of progress being made. These steps will greatly increase the likelihood of success.

Now, get a piece of paper. At the very top of the page write down the goals for the challenges or problems you're already aware of. Rank your goals from most important to least important. Work on your most important goal first. Leave space to add and rank other goals that come to mind as you read this book. Draw a line down the middle of the page. On the left-hand side of the page, underneath your goals, write: "How I and my life will be if I *don't* achieve these goals," and on the right-hand side underneath your goals write, "How I and my life will be if I *do* achieve these goals."

Now go back and fill out each half of the page with as much detail as you can. (In Appendix A, an example self-change plan is provided.) Look over the list you've constructed on each side of the page. If you're like the vast majority of students, there's much more to gain by striving to achieve your goals than by not attaining them. Read the list over daily to remind yourself of the benefits of striving towards your goals; this should help you to stick with it. Try not to focus so much on how fast you're changing, but what direction you're moving in—forward, backwards or standing still. If you find yourself moving forward, keep at what you're doing; if you find yourself moving backwards or standing still, don't abandon ship. Help is coming!

A self-change plan works much better when the self-changer is accountable to someone. So identify a Holy Spirit filled person who is supportive of what you're trying to do, and ask her or him to be your accountability partner. Give her or him a copy of your self-change plan and permission to touch base with you regularly to see how you're doing. It's important to be honest with your accountability partner about how things are going. (More than one accountability partner is okay.)

Your Backup Plan

Every self-change plan requires a contingency or backup plan; that is, what you'll do should you start faltering (making no progress or losing gains made) on your self-change plan. Faltering *doesn't* mean that you can't do it, that you're a failure, that it isn't meant to be, or that there's no hope. Faltering is just a red flag for you to assess what needs to be addressed in order for you to get back on track. The first step in your backup plan is praying for the Lord to help you identify the specific reasons why you're off-track and supply you the recommitment and drive to make the needed changes.

The second step in your backup plan is writing and reading a letter of encouragement to yourself. The letter might start off with something like: "You're reading this letter, *your name*, because you're not doing as well as you'd like in sticking to your plan to achieve your goals. It's not unusual to lose some steam from time-to-time in trying to fulfill goals, so don't be hard on yourself. You'll succeed by God's grace. Read over your list of goals and how you and your life will be when you achieve them to remind yourself of the tremendous benefit of hanging in there. Don't be discouraged, achieving goals is challenging for everyone." Write the letter in the manner most likely to rekindle your motivation.

The third step in your backup plan includes writing down everything that has stymied you. Run the obstacles by your accountability partner(s) for their observations and/or feedback.

The fourth step in your backup plan should be written statements of the *specific* things you'll do to counter the obstacle(s) identified.

The fifth step is to *act* on the specific things you wrote down to do in order to reach your goals. Let your accountability partner(s) in on your backup plan. She or he can pray for your getting back on track, help you craft the backup plan letter to yourself (as well as the third and fourth parts of your backup plan), and encourage you to progress towards your goals.

CHAPTER 2

Assess Your Vulnerability to Stress

This book is about coping with stress that can interfere with academic success; thus, it makes sense for you to measure your current vulnerability to stress. To gauge your vulnerability to stress, complete the scale below[1] by answering each question honestly with: **1**= always or almost always, **2**= usually, **3**= occasionally, **4**= almost never, **5**= never.

1. _____ I eat at least one hot, healthy meal a day.

2. _____ I get at least 8 hours of sleep most nights a week.

3. _____ When problems or challenges arise in my life, I feel able to handle them.

4. _____ I have high self-worth.

5. _____ I exercise to the point of perspiration for at least 50 minutes three times a week.

6. _____ I avoid worrying, catastrophizing, or negative thinking about challenges or problems.

7. _____ I avoid drinking alcohol or smoking.

8. _____ I avoid drinking caffeinated beverages (e.g., coffee, soda pop, energy drinks).

9. _____ I am able to forgive others and move on.

10. _____ I have enough income to meet my basic expenses/needs.

11. _____ I regularly attend wholesome social activities/events and have fun at least once a week.

12. _____ I have a network of friends I can confide in about matters that bother me.

13. _____ I avoid excessive use of food, TV, DVDs, videos, the Internet, social networking sites, video games, or other technology.

14. _____ I draw strength from my spiritual beliefs and practices.

15. _____ I am in good health, including the appropriate weight for my height.

16. _____ I am satisfied in the relationship with my significant other.

17. _____ I have sufficient energy from day-to-day.

18. _____ I am thankful for my current life situation.

19. _____ I am able to organize my time and responsibilities effectively, and keep from procrastinating.

20. _____ I take quiet time for myself during the day.

To obtain your score, add up the numbers and subtract 20. A score *over 30* suggests a vulnerability to stress. A score *between 45 and 65* suggests a serious vulnerability to stress. A score *over 65* suggests an extreme vulnerability to stress. However you scored, this book can help you.

CHAPTER 3

Work on Your General Self-Worth

Three torpedoes sink a student's academic life; one from within: low self-worth, and two from without: unhealthy relationships with someone or some activity/thing.

Let's focus on the first torpedo, low self-worth. At the root of who we are rests our self-worth: how a person *truly* thinks, believes, and feels about themselves along a continuum from a low, negative, or unhealthy self-worth to a high, positive, or healthy self-worth. It's not unusual for students to have self-worth issues, which creates difficulties not only in school, but in other life spheres as well, such as self-care, relationships, and employment. Low self-worth is stressful in and of itself because it raises levels of the stress hormone cortisol.

High or positive self-worth isn't bragging. In fact, those students who brag the most usually have the lowest self-worth. They brag in order to (1) impress others, (2) feel good about the praise they receive from broadcasting their accomplishments, and (3) convince themselves that they're somebody through hearing themselves talk about the great things they've done (things that are often exaggerations or lies).

High or positive self-worth isn't making good grades, being popular, or earning awards; it isn't having a good job, lots of money, or coming from a good family; it isn't living in a nice home or having a nice car, clothes, or other material possessions; and it isn't being "hot," a "hunk," or a good athlete. Some of the most unhappy, insecure, low self-worth students I've seen in counseling have possessed these very things. To gauge your current level of self-worth, complete the scale below by circling either "YES" or "NO."

1. I often wish I could change the way I look.
    YES/NO

2. I often worry about what others think and feel about me.
    YES/NO

3. I compare myself to others too much.
   YES/NO

4. I am overly shy or overly aggressive.
   YES/NO

5. I avoid or worry about new experiences because I fear I
   will fail.
   YES/NO

6. I often feel like I have to prove myself to others.
   YES/NO

7. I am easily hurt by criticism or respond defensively.
   YES/NO

8. I wait until the last minute before getting things done.
   YES/NO

9. I often question or feel guilty about the things I say or do.
   YES/NO

10. When I hear of others' successes or see others doing
    something better than me, I feel resentful and/or wish that
    it could have been me.
    YES/NO

11. I am too hard on myself.
    YES/NO

12. I have difficulty accepting compliments.
    YES/NO

13. I often try to act like someone I'm not, or wish I could be like
    other people I see.
    YES/NO

14. My relationships with significant others tend to be problematic.
    YES/NO

15. I don't have any spiritual beliefs or practices that help me in life.
    YES/NO

16. I am jealous, possessive, or controlling in my relationships.
    YES/NO

17. I am perfectionistic.
    YES/NO

18. I use alcohol or other drugs, technology, food, pornography, TV, video games, gambling, etc. to feel better or not so bad.
    YES/NO

19. It is very important to me to have nice clothes, a nice car, and other nice things.
    YES/NO

20. I am fearful about letting people know the "real me."
    YES/NO

21. I often brag about my accomplishments, material possessions, or other things in order to impress others.
    YES/NO

22. When people disagree with me I feel angry, resentful, or put down.
    YES/NO

23. I often go out of my way to make others happy, and neglect my own needs.
    YES/NO

24. I am critical and judgmental of others, and feel that those who make mistakes should know better.
    YES/NO

25. I feel depressed and that I can't do anything about it.
    YES/NO

If you answered "YES" to seven or more of these statements, your self-worth could probably use improvement. The strategies in this book should benefit you in this area.

Symptoms of Low Self-Worth

Here are 16 symptoms of low self-worth that can hamper academic success (and life satisfaction as well):

(1) **Constant preoccupation with yourself.** People who do this often wonder how they look, and how others think and feel about them; they feel as if something's wrong with themselves and that they just don't fit in. These types can be described as "the painfully self-conscious."

(2) **Constantly comparing yourself to others.** People who do this are typically jealous of others because, when they compare themselves to others, they always lose. The reason is because they possess a strong inferiority complex to begin with, which sets them up for falling short when comparing themselves to others. These types can be described as "the yardstick that never measures up, but down."

(3) **Difficulty receiving or accepting compliments.** People who struggle with this often feel that they shouldn't get any "strokes" or compliments because they don't believe they're worth it or deserve it. They don't believe that others who give them compliments really mean it or know what they're talking about because, "If they really knew me, they wouldn't have anything good to say about a nobody like me." These people often minimize or put down their own talents, gifts, or successes by saying things as, "It was only luck" or "It was really nothing." They may also have trouble giving "strokes" to others because of jealousy, or because they never received sufficient affirmations themselves. These types can be described as "the attention-phobic."

(4) **Chronic people-pleasers.** People who do this keep saying "yes" to requests when they really want to say "no." A person can't really feel free to say "yes" until she or he can first feel free to say "no." They tend to be overly concerned about saying or doing things that might hurt others' feelings or create conflict. These people are often driven to say and do good things for others in order to feel liked or accepted, and will go out of their way to

help people because they need to be needed; they need the "thank yous" to bolster their low self-worth. People-pleasing is overwhelming and stressful trying to keep others happy and not disappoint them, often to the neglect of one's own needs. These types can be described as "the approval dependent."

(5) **Prideful.** People who feel this way may come across with a better-than-thou attitude, but have little self-confidence or self-worth, and talk and act prideful to hide their insecurities. Their pride is just a mask over low self-worth. They may lie or exaggerate in order to bolster the view others have of them. These people tend to be rigid and self-opinionated, and unwilling to hear others out—especially when others disagree with what they think or believe. They often have an insatiable need to be right. These types can be described as "the pseudo big-headed, better than thou types."

(6) **Perfectionistic.** People like this try so hard to prove that they're so good and never make mistakes, but they're really wasting their time and effort. Because they're human, they're imperfect; and because they're imperfect, they're going to make mistakes. These people just can't let go of that drive to reach and maintain an impossible standard—a standard nobody but themselves (ultimately) pushes on them. They're driven to succeed to prove to themselves and the world that they're somebody. They can be hard to live with because of their impatience, rigidity, criticalness, nitpickiness, lecturing, irritability, and hostility toward those who don't see things the way they do or act as they want. They're also usually intolerant of others' shortcomings. These types can be described as "the I've arrived."

(7) **Jealous, possessive, and controlling in relationships with significant others.** People who feel and behave this way do so because they believe that, because they have so little to offer, they better keep that significant other nearby so she or he won't see that someone else can offer more and then, as a result, leave them. They're wracked with insecurities and fear abandonment at any moment. These people also tend to be possessive and controlling because they desperately need people around them to give them "strokes," to do things for them, to just be there so that they can feel some sense of worth. That is, relationships are a fix to help these people feel secure. These types can be described as "the I'm nobody without somebody."

(8) **Feelings of powerlessness.** People who feel this way believe they have little or no control over their life. They're partially correct. However, we can all exercise greater control over our *response* to how people treat us and to what in life comes our way. These types can be described as "the powerless-prone."

(9) **Depression.** People who feel this way may experience bouts of depression (e.g., withdrawal from family, friends, or social activities; little or no enjoyment in things that used to be pleasurable; sleeping too much or too little; eating too much because of increased appetite or eating too little because of reduced appetite; crying spells; unable to express joy; tired or low energy; concentration and memory problems; loss of interest in personal appearance; reduced self-worth; feelings of helplessness or hopelessness; suicidal thoughts or attempts). If you're considering suicide, please talk to a mental health professional immediately. Depression can also result from chronic negative thinking, unmanageable stress, when a person feels she or he is not worth much or has little to offer, or believing that others don't care about, value, or respect her or him. These types will also feel depressed over loss (death of a loved one, breakup with a significant other, flunking an exam or assignment, impairment in family relationships, peer rejection, financial instability, or a decline in health). They may indulge in self-pity. These types can be described as "the down and out."

(10) **Over-defensiveness.** People who react this way can't stand to hear constructive feedback (corrections, suggestions, opinions) from anybody because it stirs up inadequacies (negative thoughts and feelings) that they already have about themselves. They view such feedback as someone saying, "You're wrong; let me show you the right way." The real problem here is that these types are oversensitive to anything said to them because need to *always* be right and be *seen* as having it all together (which feedback threatens); feel personally attacked when given feedback or opinions; and/or they're caught up in thinking that others can see their flaws and are trying to embarrass them or put them down by giving feedback. These types can be described as "the feedback phobic."

(11) **Severe or chronic guilt feelings.** Guilt feelings in and of themselves aren't bad; they're the Holy Spirit's way of letting us know through our consciences that our motives, thoughts, feelings, words, or actions were out-of-line with His moral compass. How-

ever, for people with severe or chronic guilt issues, the guilt can pervade their thoughts to where it becomes difficult to say or do anything for fear of saying or doing something wrong. This is probably guilt from an unresolved psychological issue or Satan (both of which tend to paralyze us), and not Holy Spirit conviction, which is designed to mobilize us by inspiring confession of sin and effort to do better (repentance) in Him. These people are just too hard on themselves. These types can be described as "the guilt-ridden."

(12) **Excessive criticizing, condemning, and judging of others.** People who do this do so because, seeing imperfections in others, stir up their thoughts of superiority and the need to correct the "poor wretches" who just don't have it together as they do. These people were usually conditionally loved and/or overly criticized while growing up, and have a storehouse of resentment, anger, and bitterness that they take out on others by saying and/or doing the same hurtful things to others that were said and done to them. They genuinely believe that they're helping others by pointing out their flaws, but 99.9% of the time their words and actions only push people away. Others view them as faultfinding, and rightfully so. These types can be described as "the critical snipers."

(13) **Nervous, tense, always worrying, and avoidant of any situation that might cause anxiety.** People who feel and behave this way are often very sensitive, and tend to view strongly the world around them as dangerous. They often look for the easy way in almost every situation to avoid anxiety. These types can be described as "the on pins and needles."

(14) **Any type of addiction.** Dependency on alcohol, marijuana, tobacco, prescription or over-the-counter drugs, caffeinated beverages, pornography, romance novels, sex, food, shopping, gambling, TV, DVDs, videos, video games, the Internet, social media, watching sports, keeping busy, and even cleaning of one's place of residence can be problematic. A person isn't necessarily addicted to these "things," but to the feelings created (excitement, pleasure, some other desirable feeling) or reduced (tension, boredom, some other unpleasant feeling) by engaging in these activities. For example, compulsively cleaning and tidying is a way some use to prevent or reduce nervousness, worrying, or other uncomfortable thoughts and feelings. They experience relief not only in engaging in the act of cleaning and neatening, but in seeing things

around them clean, neat, and in order. These actions *and* seeing things clean, neat, and in order make them feel as if, "I have it all together, I'm in control, and everything is okay." But their false sense of peace is short-lived and they have to resume the compulsive cleaning and straightening again. These addicted types can be described as "the destined for disaster" because addictions never solve problems, only create new ones that together can devastate one's life. See Chapter 13 for more on addictions.

(15) **Living through others.** People who do this may follow the lives of the rich and famous (actors, actresses, athletes) in the mainstream media and put themselves in their shoes in order to derive a vicarious thrill because their own life feels so empty, boring, and unfulfilling. They may even be hooked on a soap opera. Living through others is hazardous to self-worth because the glamorous picture painted often of these celebrities and their lifestyle is not easily achieved, and so they end up feeling even more frustrated and dissatisfied. Those who live through others often depend on material possessions for happiness and try hard to project a favorable image. These types can be described as "the self-empty."

(16) **Acting like someone you're not to keep up with the Joneses.** People who act this way fear not being good enough and strive to meet the standards of others to fit in or be accepted. They try to talk and dress a certain way, accumulate certain material possessions, adopt certain attitudes, etc., so as to present an image of someone they're not in order to impress others. These types can be described as "the wanna be, but never is."

The Gist of Those with Low Self-Worth

Low self-worth is the single, most destructive force in a person's life. Those with low self-worth are starved for greater self-value. Out of desperation to feel good about themselves, they're driven to say and do things to feed that hunger. Deep down they fear that people will find out how "bad" they are, and thus will reject them, leaving them feeling even more alone and worthless than before.

Strategies to Increase Self-Worth

Here are six potent strategies to increase self-worth:

(1) Pray to God for the realization of your immense worth to Him and in Him. Remember that God created *you* and breathed the breath of life into you. He also sacrificed His Son, Jesus Christ, to pay the penalty for your sin so that you wouldn't have to die, and could live with Him forever. Oh what love and infinite value He's bestowed on us!

(2) Avoid comparing yourself to others; just focus on being the best that you can be. It takes most, if not all, of your time, energy, and effort to try to be someone else, but little if any to be yourself, because being oneself comes naturally. However, if "yourself" has shortcomings that create problems for you and others, make efforts to correct them. Do you really want to be a social chameleon, changing your image relative to the person or group you want to be like and fit in with? In time, you'll lose sight of who you really are. If you can't be the real you, people will never get to know the true you. And if people can never get to know the true you, you can never be accepted and loved for who you *really* are. One of the deepest human needs is to be accepted for who we truly are. Guess what? The One who *knows* you the best (God) loves you the *most,* and that should count for something. You mustn't base your self-worth on the opinion of others, how good you look, how you perform in life, how much education you have, how much money you make, how popular you are, whether you come from a good family or not, or how many nice things you have. Materialism is an obsessive desire for more and more and better and better things, and one is *never* satisfied. Love yourself unconditionally. If you don't accept and love yourself, it'll be hard to believe that anyone else will either.

(3) Visit a bookstore and purchase some material on building self-worth. Remember, you're looking for material that increases your realization of your *immense* worth in God's eyes, as well as His ability to work in and through your life according to His will.

(4) If you make a mistake, which *everyone* does, forgive yourself, devise a better way to handle it next time, and move on. Place your effort on a positive response to what life brings. Also, live by the serenity prayer: "God grant me the serenity to accept the things I cannot change, courage to change the things I can, and the wisdom to know the difference." Don't be so hard on yourself when things aren't going right. See where you can make improvements,

and then do it. Stop blaming yourself every time something goes wrong; at least half the time you're probably innocent.

(5) Confront your negative self-thinking or self-criticism (which is often harsher than what others might say), and worrying and catastrophizing by making a list of the positive things about yourself and your life which God has blessed you with. Read the list daily to remind yourself that there *are* good things about yourself and your life. Also, write down realistic goals for yourself, life, and service to others, along with the small steps to get there, and stick to the steps as best you can.

(6) Find a counselor or support group in order to receive help in understanding and overcoming your low self-worth. Developing a healthy self-worth can take time, so be patient. It *will* improve by God's grace.

CHAPTER 4

Discipline Yourself and Organize Your Life

Time to GO—that is, *get organized*. Lack of an organized life and self-discipline are top threats to academic success. For the purpose of this book, *organization* is defined as sound arrangement of one's daily tasks and responsibilities. *Self-discipline* is defined as doing what you've got to do, whether you feel like it or not, because it needs to be done. Self-discipline paves the way to success. Organization and self-discipline work hand in hand to increase efficiency, reduce stress, and enhance one's educational experience. If you don't TCB (take care of business), you'll soon be OOB (out of business).

God so loves things done decently and in order. There's no magic pill for disciplining yourself and organizing your life. They require self-denial, hard work, and perseverance, but the rewards are well-worth the effort. Put your will in God's hand and He will move you forward in this area. One must develop and stick to a schedule of personal devotions, eating and sleeping properly, exercise, academic study, socializing with *supportive* others (those who respect what's important to you and encourage you in it), employment if necessary, and playing sports (if you so choose *and* can spare the time). More detail about these later. Don't make too ambitious a schedule; be realistic, or give-up-itis could set in.

The Absolute Need for a Weekly Planner

A weekly planner is the *most effective* strategy to build self-discipline, get and stay organized, and achieve the balance necessary to manage a busy lifestyle. Purchase a weekly planner and use it to make a daily and/or weekly list of school and non-school tasks and responsibilities. Rank these tasks and responsibilities from *urgent* to *most important* to *least important*. Then, start with the urgent one and go down the list, crossing off each task and responsibility as you complete it. At the end of a productive day, reflect on the tasks and responsibilities accomplished, thank God for the successes, and pat yourself on the back for cooperating with God on a job well-done.

How to Put Your Weekly Planner Together

Here's how to begin to schedule in your weekly planner. Write down what time you need to be at school (or whatever the destination). Next, make a list of all the things you need to do before you can walk out the door (morning devotion, exercise, breakfast, washing-up). Beside these listed activities, write down how much time each requires. Add up all the times. This is how much time you need in the morning to get everything done before you can depart for school. Next, write down how much time it takes you to get to school and find a parking space, and add another 15 minutes (or more) should you encounter traffic or some other unforeseen circumstance. Add this time to the above figure, and you now have the total amount of time needed to do everything. For example, if your class starts at 8:00 a.m., and the total time you calculated to do everything, from morning devotion to sitting down in class—including the 15 minutes travel leeway—is two hours and 15 minutes, you need to get up at 5:45 a.m.

The next step is to write down how many hours of sleep you *must* have to wake up refreshed. For example, if you have to get up at 5:45 a.m. to do everything necessary to be sitting in class by 8:00 a.m., and you need 8 hours sleep, you must get into bed by 9:45 p.m. Now you know what time you need to get to bed at night to get a good night's rest, and what time you need to get up in the morning to complete all the things you need to do to get to class on time. Whatever time you calculated to get to bed, subtract 15 minutes—this is the time-range for your bedtime. For example, if you calculated that you need to get in bed by 9:45 p.m., subtract 15 minutes, which means your time-frame to get into bed is between 9:30 p.m. and 9:45 p.m. (Don't ask why I'm recommending that you do this; it's a secret that if divulged might undermine the benefit to you—trust me.)

Whatever time you calculated to get up in the morning, subtract 15 minutes; this is the time-frame to get up in the morning. For example, if you calculated that you need to get up at 5:45 a.m., subtract 15 minutes, which means your time-frame to get up in the morning is between 5:30 a.m. and 5:45 a.m. **Don't** oversleep.

Be sure to schedule all other daily tasks and responsibilities in your planner. You now have a schedule to go by that should prevent or reduce any stress, pressure, or rushing; that is, *if* you stick to it. In order for this schedule to work, it's imperative to get into bed within the calculated time-frame. In general, get yourself ready for tomorrow as much as possible the night before—car gassed up, homework done, book bag at the door, clothes laid out, toiletries in place, breakfast at least partially prepared, public transportation fare at hand, etc. You'll probably find yourself sitting in class 15 minutes or more ahead of schedule, relaxed, and ready to learn. You'll then have time to review the notes from the last class lecture to prime you for the one that day.

Scheduling Class Assignments

When putting in the due dates for class assignments and exams in your weekly planner, *always* schedule the due dates at least a week or more before they're actually due, thereby giving yourself extra time should you procrastinate, something unforeseen comes up that interferes with your preparation, or better still, an extra week or more to review what you've written to refine it further. Many students find it helpful to transfer the schedule in their weekly planner to a wall calendar, smartphone, or other electronic device as an additional reminder of responsibilities.

The Syllabus

If given a syllabus for a class, it's *extremely* important to read it very thoroughly, carefully, and regularly. Failure to follow the instructions/directions of the instructor often leads to unnecessary stress, and reduced academic success. Every instructor is different, so pay very close attention to what each says about their expectations. Students often ask instructors questions about class that are already answered on the syllabus or were covered during class time. Instructors don't look favorably on students who do this, thinking that they mustn't have read the syllabus or paid much attention in class. The syllabus is the class guide/map to get you from start to finish. Go through the syllabi for your classes and write down in your weekly planner or enter into your electronic device when assignments are due and exams are scheduled (again, at least a week or more early).

CHAPTER 5

Purchase the Textbook

Purchase the textbook and any other material required for the class *and* read them. Yes, funds are tight and textbooks are expensive, but you can't do your best academically if you're not familiar with the textbook and/or other material assigned by the teacher. If you absolutely can't afford the cost of a new or even used textbook for the class, partner with a fellow student or two and purchase or rent one and share it. Be careful to go in only with students who you know will be responsible about getting the book to you when it's your turn to read it.

You can also purchase many new or used textbooks online cheaply (e.g., AbeBooks.com, CheapestTextbooks.com, Half.com). Be sure to order the books well in advance of when your classes start because it sometimes takes a while for the books to arrive. Some textbooks can be purchased even cheaper as eTextbooks, or rented online (e.g., Rent-A-Text.com, Chegg.com, CampusBook Rentals.com) at a reasonable price. Some instructors will put their textbooks and/or other required reading on reserve in the school library, but this is rare (it doesn't hurt to ask an instructor if she or he will put their course material on reserve). However, even when the textbook and/or other material is available on reserve, they're often not available for check-out when you need them and you're usually allowed access to the material only for a limited time.

CHAPTER 6

Don't Procrastinate

Procrastination is a dagger in the back of academic success causing students unnecessary stress and hemorrhaging their potential. Procrastination specific to academics is delaying or avoiding studying for an exam, writing a paper, or completing some other assignment until the last moment. Then, there's so much to do and little time to do it in. Procrastination is academic suicide, and the single most common reason why students are stressed out, dissatisfied with their academic experience, and perform below their potential. All of which can lead to settling for mediocre performance, or dropping out of classes or school. Aren't you tired of feeling under pressure and stressed when exams come around or major assignments beome due? Why put off studying until later when you have the time to do it now? Studying is more enjoyable and effective when done in a relaxed manner. Stay on top of your studies or they'll pile up on you and crush academic success. Procrastination can undermine your career potential, if you carry it into the workplace.

The Top Five Reasons Students Procrastinate

The top five reasons students procrastinate are:
    (1) Believing "I still have time."
    (2) Thinking "I can't get going until I have to."
    (3) Fearfulness or anxiety about assignments and/or tests.
    (4) Lack of self-discipline or disorganization.
    (5) Lack of clarity or understanding about an assignment.

Number 1: Believing "I still have time." Do you really enjoy working "under the gun?" This belief is the most damaging of the five to academic success. These students truly believe that there's still plenty of time to write that paper or study for that exam as the clock ticks down to the deadline. It's very common for these types of students to wait until the weekend before an assignment is due, or an exam, to begin preparation. Believing that you still have time holds academic performance and satisfaction hostage, and there's no escape unless one makes significant effort to break free.

Number 2: Thinking "I can't get going until I have to." Far too many students procrastinate simply because they can't seem to muster the drive to prepare well in advance for an exam or assignment. Many students voice little desire to tackle an assignment or study for an exam until the deadline is upon them; then they feel a burst of *desperate* motivation to get going. Waiting until the last minute, when the pressure is on, can become habitual and lead to a cycle of procrastination in every class. Don't wait until the final exam to get serious about studying. By then it's often too late.

Number 3: "Fearfulness or anxiety about assignments and/or tests." Test/academic performance anxiety is common among students at all educational levels. The reasons are myriad, but the two most common are low academic self-confidence and poor preparation. Those with little confidence when it comes to academic performance often feel that no matter how hard they try, *failure* is the likely outcome. Studying is painful, overwhelming, and seems hopeless; many find it easier to cope with demanding schoolwork *by just not doing it*. Should you score poorly on the *first* exam or assignment in a class, try not to be so discouraged that you drop the class. See where you need to improve, and then get help to make the needed change(s). You don't have to be *smart* to do well in school, just be a *hard worker*. School isn't easy, but just as lifting weights a tad heavier than what one is ready for strengthens muscle, so the challenge to grasp complex academic material outside one's mental comfort zone enhances intellectual fortitude.

These types of students can benefit from counseling to explore the origins of their fragile academic self-confidence and learn strategies to counter the obstacles that get in the way of greater comfort with assignments and tests. Regarding poor preparation: if you don't put in the time necessary to complete the assignment or study for the exam, you'll be stressed out, perform below your potential, and be dissatisfied with your academic experience.

Number 4: "Lack of self-discipline or disorganization." This shortcoming was addressed earlier in Chapter 4 above, "Discipline Yourself and Organize Your Life."

Number 5: "Lack of clarity or understanding about the assignment." It's difficult to start an assignment if you have little to no idea about what you're supposed to do or how you're supposed to do it. If the syllabus and/or instructor clearly spells out how the assignment should be done, there should be no confusion. But in those instances where the syllabus or instructor isn't clear, or you need more direction, try these. Ask the instructor for greater clarity and/or for examples of the assignments you can review to get a better idea of what you should be doing. You can also consult the "brainiacs" in your class who always seem to know what's going on. Lastly, you can seek out former students of your instructor's classes to gain an idea of what she or he is looking for.

Some Other Reasons Why Students Procrastinate

Additionally, some students procrastinate because they're too busy with other things to get assignments or studying done promptly, find little to no interest, energy, or enjoyment in school assignments or tests, feel overwhelmed by the preparation necessary for the assignment or test, or don't like school or the teacher. Others don't realize that school is a full-time job or commitment. Some don't take their classes serious enough, avoid or minimize taking responsibility for their learning, or expect school to be easier than it actually is. Some expect teacher mercy, grace, or extra credit assignments to make up for their poor academic effort or laziness.

Students may also procrastinate because their motives for being in school are less than ideal to sustain interest and motivation to study diligently. Here are some less than ideal motives students give for going to college: (1) their friends are continuing on in school, so they might as well also; (2) feeling that there's nothing else to do, so why not enroll; (3) not feeling ready or willing to be self-reliant (e.g., get a job, get one's own place, pay one's bills); (4) only wanting to participate in the fun stuff, which doesn't (in their opinion) include studying; (5) their parents giving them the ultimatum of continuing on in school or finding another place to live; (6) go only to please their parents; (7) wanting to escape a bad family situation; and/or (8) financial aid is available (which they intend to use for *non-school related* expenses). You've got to want the degree for yourself, not for your parents, relatives, or a teacher.

It's okay if some of the motivation to pursue your education is prompted by the encouragement of others, but the primary reason should be because *you* want it. There should be some sense that obtaining an education is for a meaningful purpose (i.e., you have an idea of the type of career the Lord has called you to and the education required). If the motivation issue seems related to just not knowing what career to pursue, earnestly pray to the Lord to reveal His plan for your life.

Also, talk to an academic counselor and/or complete a career questionnaire to help identify areas of career interest and ability. Remember, you can always take the courses everybody has to take (General Education) while deciding on a major or career. Whatever the motivation, it's important for *you* to know *why* you're going to school. If your motive for attending school is other than desirable, when things get tough your stress will likely increase and perseverance wane. In the end, if you *have* to go to school, why not make the best of it? Strive to learn as much as you can in every class rather than the minimum amount needed to pass the class.

Strategies to Overcome Procrastination and Increase Study Effectiveness

So, what are some techniques to overcome procrastination and increase study effectiveness?

(1) Pray for power to rid your academic life of procrastination and increase your study effectiveness. God **will** most certainly supply your need here because He wants you to be maximally prepared for His calling.

(2) Block off times in your weekly planner devoted to studying, and stick to them no matter what. In many schools the motto is "Party now, Study later." Avoid this practice as you would a 16-wheeler barreling down on you. You can't enjoy fully hanging out with friends or any recreational activity when you *know* you have studying to do. Why not get your studying out of the way and *then* enjoy yourself? You'll be free of guilt and have greater fun knowing that you're current on your studies.

(3) Devise and employ sound study habits. More specifically, start doing the reading and writing up of flashcards, applying rote rehearsal, elaborative rehearsal (linking or relating new information with something you already know), mnemonics (coming up with an acronym to remember information), or whatever works for

you now relative to the course material to study from. Unless you have classes back-to-back or some other appointment after a class, why not immediately start on your homework while much is still fresh in your mind? If you do this regularly for each class, along with other blocked off periods of studying, all you'll need to study before each exam are the notes your instructors give the last lecture before the exam. This is a much more manageable amount of material to study than a backlog of lectures and book chapters from procrastinating. Also, students tend to study their *best* for the *final* exam. Study for the *first* exam, and all other exams, like you would for the final exam. Effective study promotes increased learning and academic enjoyment, which facilitates realized potential.

(4) Find a place free of distractions to study (in your car at a park, a quiet corner in the library, an empty classroom, way up on top of a football stadium, in your bedroom with the door bolted and a sentry posted outside). Also, shut down your computer, switch your smartphone off, and turn the television to the wall (or dispensed with altogether if necessary)—so you can focus without interruption. Sometimes, while trying to study, thoughts of things to do can come up and derail you. No need to worry; just keep a notepad and pen or voice recorder nearby, jot down or voice record the thoughts, and tend to them after the study session.

(5) Clean and straighten up your place of study. A messy study environment can undermine feeling organized.

(6) Let your friends and family know that you don't want to be disturbed during your study times, and stand firm if anyone attempts to draw you away from your study periods.

(7) Consider a study partner or study group (with only those serious about *studying*).

(8) Don't get into the cramming habit; this only increases *fear of failure*, reduces study effectiveness, and leads to retention of information for just the short term. Sure, there'll be times when you can get a decent grade despite cramming, but don't be fooled; cramming won't work the higher you climb the educational ladder.

(9) Stay relaxed when studying and reduce life stress in general. The more tense you are when studying, the less likely you'll be able to store information. You might try some relaxation techniques before studying. If your life is chaotic/too busy, you'll probably have to make some major changes to be able to study without

preoccupation with juggling multiple responsibilities.

(10) Sleep at least 8 hours a night. If you're fighting drowsiness when trying to study, take a brisk 5-10 minute walk or splash cold water on your face. If these don't rouse you, close the book, take a nap, then get back to work. Studying done while fatigued probably won't stick, so you'll have wasted time and effort.

(11) Use it or lose it; that is, your general memory ability on a regular basis. For example, next time you have to go shopping at the supermarket, first make a shopping list, then memorize it as best you can and stuff it in your pocket. Proceed to shop until you believe you've purchased everything on your list. Then, while in the long check-out line, review the items in your cart to see if they match your memory of what's on the shopping list. Now pull out the list and see if you've got everything. Continue this practice for as long as you live. You can also improve your memory ability by writing down or entering into your smartphone the names, phone numbers, addresses, etc. given you, and memorizing them as best you can. Then, later on at home try to recall them; check your accuracy against what you have on record. Another good exercise to improve your memory is to memorize verses in the Bible. In time, you'll be amazed at how accurate your recall becomes.

(12) Regularly spend time in the tutoring center or any support services at your school. Why not take advantage of the help? Plus, these services provide accountability to take school seriously.

(13) Although it's natural to resist these next two suggestions, they're much too effective in countering procrastination to fight against. Whatever date an instructor says an assignment is due, schedule it to be due *a week or more early.* By doing so you can turn in the assignment early (which can't but help your reputation in the instructor's eyes); or, if some unforeseen circumstance arises, you'll still have a week or more to complete the assignment and fine tune it. Also, whatever date an exam is scheduled to take place on, bump it back at least a week earlier. This way, you'll have an extra week to further reinforce the test material you're *already* familiar with.

It's *never* too early to begin studying. Once you overcome procrastination, you'll experience what few students ever come to know: academic bliss—the sense of peace and control of academics because you've done what you've needed to do on time, if not ahead of schedule. You'll never want to go back to the old ways.

CHAPTER 7

No Grade Perfectionism

Please don't make "As" your idol or you'll become caught up in the driven, obsessive, and joyless pursuit of them. You *don't* have to get straight "As" to be a success. Just pray for success, work hard in harmony with the prayer, don't give up, and ask the right people (those already where you want to go or who hire or admit where you want to be) the right questions (e.g., "How did you get where you are?" "What qualifications are you looking for in the people you hire or accept in your program?"), and do as they say. Of course, any recommendations that are immoral, unethical, illegal, neglect self-care, and/or are detrimental to others shouldn't be carried out. You can sleep much better knowing that you got where you wanted with strict integrity and sound health.

Many students are concerned with only one thing—getting "As." Often, these students have little desire to understand or master the material beyond the short term—"spitting it out" on the exam to get a good grade—and, if given the same exam a day or two later, they'd very likely score lower. Though nothing is wrong with wanting good grades, the priority of the educational experience should be ALS (actually learning something), and *not* just getting a high GPA (grade point average). You should go to school with the desire to learn, and to better yourself, others, and the world around you according to God's will. Too much emphasis has been placed on the GPA to the detriment of ALS, resulting in many students being so stressed out over academic performance that they seek to escape the pressure through abuse of, or addiction to, alcohol and other drugs and/or activities. Some even resort to suicide.

The students who worship grades are often stressed, worried, and dissatisfied with their educational experience. They're driven, class after class, semester after semester, year after year, to make the grade. To these students, anything less than an "A" is an "F." Some, out of desperation for a higher grade, will resort to cheating or feigning illness or emergency to qualify for a make up exam, thereby allowing more time to study for the exam and/or get with a classmate about what was on the exam. Some of the extremely desperate will offer sexual favors for a boosted grade. In these cases, deeper issues are indicated, as is need of immediate attention by a counselor.

Many academic perfectionists get ill around midterms and finals, likely due to increased stress to perform, which weakens their immune system.[2] Academic perfectionists also tend to sacrifice health around exam time or when a major assignment is due, which may also contribute to weakening of their immune systems. The academically lax are typically less stressed around midterms and finals, and rarely neglect themselves because they don't equate their academic success with personal value and future achievement nearly as much as do academic perfectionists. Academic perfectionists would experience much less stress and greater satisfaction with their studies if they'd realize that the goal isn't to be the best, but to do the best you can.

The desire for high grades shouldn't supersede acquiring motivation, insights, knowledge, and skills to draw on for the long term. Imagine if the last time the surgeon, about to cut you open, picked up a journal on surgical techniques was when she or he prepared to take their medical boards years ago. You'd probably feel more comfortable and, certainly, better served by a surgeon who regularly reads surgical journals and participates in other knowledge and skill-enhancing activities related to her or his work.

Some students are driven to excel because parents, out of a variety motives, have almost traumatized them about the need to succeed. These motives can be (1) legitimate (just wanting their children to reach their fullest potential); (2) selfish (living through their children's successes resulting in zero tolerance for anything but grade perfection); (3) roughshod (insensitive to the effects of the pressure they're putting on their children, ignoring or minimizing what their children's interests might be); (4) competitive (wanting their children to do as well, if not better, than other children who are excelling); or (5) oblivious (lack of awareness or denial that their child—or the academic environment in some cases —has deficiencies that impede academic success).

Parents mean well in encouraging their children to excel academically, but they can sometimes be so demanding that the pressure backfires and their children perform worse. And when they fall short of their parents' expectations, they believe they've failed their parents and will never be good enough to them. Some children may develop anger and resentment towards their parents and act up, creating parent-child conflict. No parental efforts to see a son or daughter achieve academically are worth the impairment of emotional health and/or the parent-child relationship.

Are You An Academic Perfectionist?

Not sure if you're an academic perfectionist? Fill out the following questionnaire[3] below by circling "T" for true and "F" for false, and see for yourself:

1. T F It is difficult for me to relax.

2. T F People think I'm smart, but inside I really don't feel that way.

3. T F My parents or other people will think less of me if I make a mistake or fail.

4. T F I tend to become self-critical, think less of myself, or get upset when I make a mistake or fail in some way.

5. T F If I don't set the highest standards for myself, I would probably get lazy and end up a nobody.

6. T F An average performance is unsatisfying to me; I believe I should have done better.

7. T F School is very stressful for me.

8. T F I feel I must make "A" grades.

9. T F The only time I seem to feel any real satisfaction or joy in life is when I've done something very well.

10. T F If I get down on myself for failing to live up to my expectations, it'll help me to do better in the future.

If you answered "T" (true) for more than five of these statements, then you're likely an academic perfectionist, and could benefit from counseling to identify the relationships between your drive to perform perfectly academically and your feelings of self-worth, future success, and/or other insecurities.

CHAPTER 8

Practice Classroom Etiquette

Conduct yourself in a responsible manner in your classes to avoid unnecessarily irritating the instructor. Come to class on time every time, and stay the full-time. Most instructors tend to think unfavorably about students with chronic attendance problems. And avoid being tardy or absent on an exam day or when a major assignment is due; many instructors can't help but think that you procrastinated and pushed the limit for more time to study or complete an assignment. When entering or exiting the class, do so quietly and refrain from walking in between the instructor and the class. If an instructor doesn't say how she or he would like to be addressed, ask. Then, make sure to address her or him that way.

Also, sit as close to the front of the class as possible. Teachers tend to believe that front-row students are serious about their classes. This isn't always true, there are serious students who sit elsewhere; however, why not take advantage of this perception, and make sure you live up to it.

Don't ask the instructor for a stapler, pen, or anything that you should've already taken care of, as the instructor is likely to peg you as unprepared and disorganized. Refrain from side conversations, checking social media, your e-mail, texting, tweeting, or surfing the Internet during class time. If the instructor discovers you doing this, your standing could be tainted. Turn off any electronic device unless using it to take notes or for other legitimate class purposes.

Don't use class time to copy notes from a missed class; instructors want your full attention, and copying notes from a previous lecture implies disrespect for the instructor and/or disinterest in what the instructor has to say. (Even if this is true, do you want the instructor to know?)

Please respect others' thoughts, beliefs, and feelings in class—just as you would like others to do for you. Avoid inappropriate self-disclosure or questions. Unless the instructor gives permission, avoid eating or drinking in class. Teachers typically

45

appreciate student participation in class discussions, so try to contribute regularly. However, don't overdo your participation. Teachers aren't especially fond of students who always have a comment or question on everything. Think quality, not quantity.

Even though you may be shy, concerned about saying the wrong thing, or feel like you're not smart enough, it's a good idea to push yourself to get involved in class discussions and activities. Be sure to raise your hand high enough to be seen by the instructor, and when called upon speak clearly and loud enough to be understood. Also, ask questions when you don't understand something. You can also go to the teacher's office or use e-mail. Students feel much better about themselves and classes when they ask questions and/or make comments.

Don't wait until you *feel* like it to participate; it may never happen. Speak up and let your feelings catch up with your participation. The more you contribute to class discussions, the easier it gets. However, don't expect total comfort; some of the best orators report bouts of public speaking discomfort. Remember, doing what you need to do, even when you don't feel like doing it, is a principle that should be applied to any situation in life, especially where trepidation to speak rears up.

Refrain from excessive daydreaming or fantasizing in class. They're essentially mental escapes (from something in the here and now that is boring, unfulfilling, or unpleasant) into one's private world of reminiscing, make-believe, or imagining the possible outcome(s) of an event. While daydreaming or fantasizing isn't necessarily bad, if done excessively in class it can cause you to miss out on needed information. (Plus, if your teacher notices that glazed, faraway look in your eyes, she or he may think that you're on drugs or find the class boring).

Avoid chronic clock-watching; it gives the impression that you can't wait for class to end. By all means, *don't fall asleep on the teacher or give one of those yawns she or he can hear from across the room.* If an instructor offers extra points or any benefit for good attendance, regular class participation, turning in assignments early, involvement in outside class activities, etc., jump on it like you would a $100 bill blowing across your path. Why wouldn't a student *rush* to take advantage of these opportunities designed to help her or him grade-wise? Unfortunately, there are students who don't take advantage of these opportunities which is neglectful at least, inexcusable at most, and boggles an instructor's mind. To pass up such opportunities might be viewed by an instructor as academic lethargy or worse.

Avoid dropping in to see an instructor outside of her or his office hours. The instructor may view your stopping by as an intrusion. Teachers are busy people, just like students, and need downtime to rejuvenate. When visiting an instructor during her or his office hours, keep the meeting as brief as possible by getting right to the point. The instructor will very much appreciate your responsible use of their time.

Avoid asking a teacher "What do I need to do to pass the class?" Most teachers believe that when a student asks this type of question it's to find out the *minimum* amount of work necessary to get by. This will likely leave a poor impression with the teacher of the student's willingness to put forth *maximum* effort into the class. Also, if you miss a class, don't ask "Did I miss anything important?" The teacher is likely to be annoyed, if not offended, by this question because in 99.9% of teachers' minds, every class is important. Don't ever blow-off an assignment or exam. This is a sure-fire way to aggravate a teacher to no end. It's better to turn in a poorly done assignment or take an exam you're not prepared for than to turn in no assignment at all or not show up for an exam. And refrain from asking a teacher how many times you've been absent or tardy, if they're included in their grading system, or what your scores on exams or assignments are. You *should* know this information if you're taking school seriously by keeping such records.

Also, while teachers want only the best for their students, never let them be able to say that they want more for you than you want for yourself, or that they work harder for you than you do for yourself. Set high expectations (but not unreasonable ones) for yourself. Then, work as hard, if not harder than your teachers to achieve them. In general, be conscientious in all things from the outset of class. You won't be sorry you did.

CHAPTER 9

Speak to the Instructor Before
Any Problems Get Out of Hand

It's a good idea to touch base with your instructors at the beginning of each semester or school year so that they can begin to attach a face to your name. However, be careful not to come across as trying to earn brownie points. It's very important to make appointments with your instructors *before* any problems get out of hand; this can go a long way to prevent stress from becoming overwhelming. It's also important to arrive *on time* for the appointments with your instructors. Few things tick off instructors more than students who don't show, or who are late for appointments. If you can't make the appointment or are running late, contact the instructor ASAP.

Let your instructors know if you have a disability. The American Disabilities Act (ADA) requires that students with disabilities be reasonably accommodated with extra time to complete exams, a distraction-free environment, the use audio recording devices or note-takers, etc. (depending on the disability). You may first need to contact the Disability Center or similar such organization on your campus before approaching instructors.

Most importantly, don't wait until the end of the semester or school year to inform your instructors about challenges or problems. Most instructors are willing to help students if they're approached early on about any concerns. When the problem is the instructor or class itself, it can be very stressful, if not terrifying. Pray before you say or do anything. Then, make absolutely certain that you're not to blame for the predicament (or at least that you've done all you can to shore up where you fell short), and then think through what you want to say. Whatever you say, remember that some instructors have fragile to big egos. They can get defensive when a finger is even slightly pointed their way, so package your conversation with respect and tact. You may want to preface any concerns you have about the class with some positives in order to come across with a balanced view of your class experience.

If the instructor should point out areas in need of improvement on your part, don't get defensive, or take it to mean that you're a bad student or the instructor dislikes you. View it, instead, as the instructor believing that you're capable of better, and wanting to see you reach your fullest potential. If this effort fails to bring about the needed changes, follow the next step in school protocol to address student problems with instructors, which typically involves making an appointment with the teacher's supervisor.

CHAPTER 10

Be Careful in Your Relationships with Significant Others and Peers

Most people seem to cling to one of two extremes: either putting self first to the neglect of others (the most common), or putting others first to the neglect of self. Both extremes cause stress. Choosing God first will put self and others in proper perspective and reduce stress. There's, of course, nothing wrong with spending time with that significant other, but never to the neglect of self, other people, or important activities. If you spend so much time with her or him that you neglect self, other people or important activities, then perhaps now isn't the time to be romantically involved. (It's no more appropriate to spend hardly any time with someone you care for than it is to spend *all* your time with her or him— there must be a healthy balance.) The majority of students who "constellate" around someone, to the neglect of other important people and areas of their life, tend to be more insecure, lonely, and devastated by a breakup than those students who don't neglect other aspects of their lives.

Please, don't give your heart *totally* to anyone but God. He's the only One that your heart will be completely safe with. These students would do well to take a "fast" (break) from romantic relationships for an extended period of time in order to focus on becoming more secure within themselves. Counseling is indicated when a student feels depressed if not in a significant relationship.

When the Relationship with a Significant Other is Unhealthy

Chapter 3, "Work on Your General Self-Worth" discusses one of the three torpedoes that sink a student's academic life, that from within: low self-worth. The second torpedo, that from without, is an unhealthy relationship with someone, which will detract from academic success in a profound way because of the relationship chaos and highly charged emotions involved. An unhealthy relationship can include belittling of your spiritual or other priorities, verbal or physical abuse, jealousy, possessiveness, controlling, unfaithfulness, unmet essential needs, chronically poor communication, irresponsibility, or any other negativity. If you've been appropriately assertive (see Chapter 11, "Be Appropriately Assertive") in expressing your thoughts, feelings, and expectations about the problematic relationship, and no improvement has occurred, *get out!* Too many students stay in a relationship past the expiration date.

If you stay in the relationship with someone who engages in wrong words and behavior and has *no* intention of changing, she or he will feel more and more that their behavior is okay or not that bad because you're *still* with her or him. Don't put up with it. It's not worth your self-respect and happiness. Try not to view the breakup of a bad relationship as losing someone you love or a failure on your part. View it instead as an opportunity to gain greater peace. No matter how much you want to be with someone you care for, don't ignore the red flags in your relationship, that gut feeling, or those things said or done by one or both of you that cause you to sense something's very wrong here.

Also, don't be so quick to dismiss the feedback about your relationship from those who care about you and you can trust (e.g., parents, pastor, best friend); there's probably some truth you need to hear, accept, and act upon. If both of you in the relationship don't recognize that there are problems, how can they be solved? Even worse, some students would rather be in a bad relationship than in none at all. Female students especially must avoid staying in a bad relationship because they tend to be more negatively affected or damaged by a troubled relationship.

Students who stay in bad relationships tend to have lower self-worth, higher levels of clinginess/neediness, and are more terrified of being alone than those who don't stay. They're often submissive to avoid rejection/abandonment, *intensely* attached to their significant other (needing to be with her or him all the time so as not to lose the connection and in love feeling), and believe that whoever they're with is the best they can get—so they hold on desperately to the relationship. This can lead to putting up with abuse (and unhappiness) in their relationships. Those who stay in bad relationships also tend to say and/or do things that sabotage their relationships, to dislike themselves and, in some instances, to hate and reject who they are. In these cases, intimate relationships should be avoided and counseling sought. *How can you take care of the relationship with your significant other if you can't even take care of the relationship with yourself? Love yourself, and stop looking for someone to love you.*

These students tend to struggle with codependency (preoccupied with, overly responsible for, and hypersensitive to others' needs, wants, feelings, and behavior to the neglect of their own), thus setting themselves up to be controlled by others or controlling of others. People-pleasing and poor assertiveness are common among those with codependency. The codependent person tends to feel good about her- or himself and life *only* when the person she or he is involved with feels good about her- or himself and life. This preoccupation with another person and their life can lead to all types of negative behavior.

Are You Codependent?

Not sure if you're codependent or not? Fill out the survey below[4] and find out for yourself.

1. YES NO I feel responsible for other people's feelings and actions.

2. YES NO I have low self-worth or insecurities.

3. YES NO It is very important to me that people like and approve of me.

4. YES NO I try to anticipate other people's needs.

5. YES NO I often say "yes" when I really want to say "no."

6. YES NO I become easily absorbed in the pain and problems of other people.

7. YES NO I tend to go overboard in trying to please or help people to the neglect of my own needs.

8. YES NO I feel sad or angry because I give so much to others and they give so little back.

9. YES   NO   I feel uncomfortable or guilty when someone gives to me.

10. YES   NO   I am often in relationships with needy people, or needy people are attracted to me.

11. YES   NO   I worry a great deal about my relationships working out.

12. YES   NO   I feel angry, victimized, unappreciated, and used in my relationships with others.

13. YES   NO   I fear making mistakes and blame myself for most things that go wrong.

14. YES   NO   I often try to control people.

15. YES   NO   I tend to ignore relationship problems or act like the problems are not really that bad.

16. YES   NO   I seem to be the only one putting time and energy into the relationship with my significant other.

17. YES   NO   I become very scared at the thought of losing someone because I don't like being alone, and will do almost anything to hold on to a relationship.

18. YES   NO   I have major trouble being assertive in my relationships.

19. YES   NO   I tend to stay in relationships that aren't very good or positive.

20. YES   NO   I am very uncomfortable and frightened by others' anger.

If you answered "YES" to five or more of these statements, you may have a problem with codependency. Apply the strategies in the section below to maximize entering into and maintaining a healthy (non-codependent) relationship, *and* please give counseling a try.

Strategies to Maximize Entering into and Maintaining a Healthy (Non-Codependent) Relationship

Here are 13 effective techniques to maximize entering into and maintaining a healthy (non-codependent) relationship:

(1) Choose as your first priority to keep your personal relationship with Jesus Christ vibrant through regular prayer, Bible study, and serving others. A strong personal relationship with Jesus Christ will go a long way to prevent a "desperate" need for someone in your life, because His presence fills that space in your heart designed by Him for Him to provide your deepest needs.

(2) Work on your self-worth (see Chapter 3, "Work on Your General Self-Worth"). The better you feel about yourself the less likely unhealthy thoughts, feelings, and behaviors will emerge in your relationships. Also, just because not having a relationship *feels* intolerable, don't compromise your values in order to please someone or prevent someone from leaving you. Don't look for your greatest fulfillment in interpersonal relationships. Real fulfillment primarily comes from realizing your *immeasurable* worth in God's eyes, His love for you, and living out His will in your life.

(3) Shake before you date. When someone invites you out for a date, ask "Why me?" (or some other similar question) in order to begin to get a feel for why this person is interested in going out with you, given all the possibilities out there. If their response isn't forthcoming, or seems rather superficial or suspicious, you can always say something like, "No thank you, right now I'm not dating," or "Thanks for your interest (or asking), but I'm juggling a lot right now that needs my full attention." In such situations, don't ignore your gut feelings if they've historically proven accurate.

Of course, with whatever answer you give other than "yes," you'll be opening yourself up for other questions. You're not obligated to answer them. Oftentimes people ask "why" or other "explain to me your rationale for saying no to me" type questions to try and counter or pick apart your refusal, which tells you that perhaps their priority isn't respecting your decision but simply pressing their agenda. If you say "yes" to a date, you might want to voice kindly your "no-no" list—those things you absolutely won't tolerate on a date and/or in a relationship (e.g., name-calling, sexual innuendos or sexual activity pressure, asking for money, controlling behavior, alcohol or other drug use, etc).

The preceding suggestion seems rather risky, and may make you feel uncomfortable, but—after hearing your "no-no" list—many of the types with relationship issues or hidden agendas about asking you out for a date will either slink away, realizing that you're not easy prey or someone who'll put up with their games, or it will compel them to self-check their ability to measure up to someone with enough self-respect to state their standards.

(4) Pray for, *don't prey on*, one another. It's important when dating to not prey on one another, but to *pray for* one another. This helps reduce any relationship shenanigans.

(5) Think essentialism. Identify the one, two, and no more than three essentials in a serious relationship for you to be satisfied. Discuss with the person whether she or he is willing or able to deliver them. If she or he is unwilling or unable, consider letting the relationship go no further than being acquaintances or friends, or ending the relationship right there. Also, be honest with yourself about *your* willingness and ability to meet *their* expectations. If being honest with yourself leads to the conclusion that you're not able to deliver, be up front about it, and seek through prayer what to do next. However, if she or he expresses any "essentials" that God wouldn't approve of or are unreasonable, you should voice this concern and not allow the relationship to deepen.

(6) Regularly check your "needy meter." When neediness is high, so is sensitivity to everything in your relationships. This can lead to misinterpretations, emotional upheaval, fears of rejection or abandonment, and tolerating abuse by others.

(7) Try not to move so fast in your intimate relationships; shed this practice as you would a jacket on fire. If you find yourself moving too fast, you're probably feeling insecure about yourself or the relationship, and may be pressing for quick intimacy in order to feel more confident that the other person accepts you, or that the relationship is genuine. It's very risky to move fast because your significant other may feel uncomfortable, smothered, or pressured,

and may either break things off or exploit your vulnerability. Also, avoid any sexual talk or activity (e.g., sexual innuendos or discussions via "sexting"—texting that is sexual in nature—or face-to-face, kissing, fondling, oral sex, sexual intercourse). These activities very often lead to the relationship being centered around sexual activity to the neglect of the important aspects of the dating relationship (e.g., building a strong friendship, praying and studying the Bible together, focusing on school work).

(8) Keep a balance in terms of give and take. Don't look out for and second guess her or his needs so much that you neglect yourself. Also, don't be controlling or demanding; it'll only turn her or him off and push her or him away.

(9) Don't be so frightened of hurting people's feelings that this fear gets in the way of being appropriately assertive. If someone says or does something to you out of line, speak up for yourself straightforwardly and tactfully.

(10) Don't automatically view your significant other's disappointment as indication that you've failed or are to blame. It's easy for people to blame the other, lay "guilt trips," and manipulate. Don't be a victim of this; and make sure that you're not a victimizer yourself.

(11) Stay in your own emotional backyard. Your responsibility is to manage *your* emotional and behavioral reactions, not anyone else's. How can you even begin to manage another's emotions and behavior when controlling your own can be as difficult as breaking a bronco on steroids?

(12) Identify your unmet need(s). Realize that 99% of the time when you get bent out of shape over someone not responding to you the way you want, it's probably because you have some unmet need that you're not aware of and you're trying to fulfill it through their behavior.

(13) Get relationship help. Consider personal counseling, participating in a self-help group such as Co-Dependents Anonymous, or a group therapy focusing on relationship conflicts.

Dealing with a Painful Breakup

One of the most painful experiences students report is the breakup of a relationship. The pain can be so severe that interest in school is abandoned. If there was sexual activity in the relationship, the pain over the loss can be overwhelming because more intense feelings have been involved. The pain of a breakup is usually felt more keenly by females than by males, primarily because females tend to invest more of themselves in relationships, to define their self-worth based on the absence or presence of a relationship, and to be more sensitive about relationships in general. Of course there are many exceptions to these tendencies.

To minimize entering into a new relationship *before* you've recovered from a painful breakup, make sure to apply the following four-step strategy: pray, delay, weigh, and take it day-by-day.

Pray that the Lord enables you to endure the pain of the breakup and learn from the previous relationship. He will certainly meet your need here because God is in the growth-promoting business, and desires us to be prepared for future trials.

Delay entering into a new relationship until you're no longer absorbed in the thoughts and feelings of the old one. Expect that you'll miss the person that you broke up with (sometimes so much that it feels impossible to live without her or him), but *don't* let it cause you to get back with her or him—don't call, text, stalk, or drop in on her or him. It *was* the right decision to get out. And please don't make the mistake that many students make of trying to get over an old relationship with a new one. Rebound relationships rarely work out; all you'll end up doing is delaying or bypassing the healing process and wishing the person you're currently seeing was the one you broke up with. It can take 6 months or longer to recover fully from a painful breakup. No matter how lonely or empty you feel following the breakup, give yourself time to heal (which may require counseling) before considering another relationship. Trust in the opposite sex is often damaged following a relationship breakup, and must be given time to be restored.

Weigh honestly the contribution *you* and the "ex" made to the breakup, what damage it has done to you personally, and what you might do differently in a future relationship. You might want to write down what you discover from your search as ready reminders for the future.

Take it day-by-day by saying to yourself, "I must take it a day at a time regarding how I'm going to handle my thoughts and feelings about this breakup, and not worry about how I'm going to make it through the rest of my life." If you shun this recovery process, you risk reaching back for the old relationship or bringing baggage from the old relationship into the new one, which will create problems.

After recovery from the old relationship, make sure to be strong enough to accept nothing less in any future relationship than better than what you already had. Don't lower your standards. Don't repeat the *same* mistake. This next suggestion is tough to do, but in order to heal and move on, it's necessary to forgive those who have hurt or angered you. Forgiveness doesn't mean that you're accepting, excusing, or minimizing what was said or done to you. Forgiveness is "letting go" of the negative thoughts, feelings, and behaviors toward someone who you believe has treated you unjustly. Forgiveness results in closure (feeling emotionally at peace) relative to the predicament. Not forgiving, or holding on to the negative thoughts (obsessing over the incident, conjuring up ways to seek revenge) and feelings (resentment, anger) only increases your risk of developing hypertension, distrust, depression, and/or anxiety.[5,6] Worse, as you suffer through all this, the party you blame for what you're going through has gone on with her or his life. You're hurting no one but yourself, so why not let it all go? The benefits of letting go far outweigh any perceived benefits of holding on. And don't look back, it's gone for a reason.

This state of forgiveness is achieved ideally by discussing your thoughts and feelings with the one who hurt or angered you. If you're responsible, even in the smallest part for the breakup, you might begin by saying, "I'm sorry for what I said (or did) that hurt (or angered) you." You're not excusing your ex's role in the breakup; you're just acknowledging your part, which often softens the other party to confess their contribution. When talking with the ex isn't possible or safe, try talking with a good friend or counselor, or joining a support group focused on overcoming the pain of a breakup and facilitating the forgiveness process.

A 2009 study showed that praying for the relationship partner one is having problems with increases one's willingness to forgive.[7] If praying doesn't enable forgiveness, seek a pastoral counselor for help. Keep in mind that it often takes time for most people to truly forgive (and let go of hard feelings).

Hanging Out Can Hang You Up Academically

Excessive hanging out with a significant other or peers is another big threat to an academically successful experience. It's okay to spend time with a special someone or friends, but make sure it doesn't consume time needed for other responsibilities. Also, make sure that the special someone or peers you hang out with are supportive of your academics. If, after you've emphasized your need to study, anyone persists in trying to persuade you to push your studies aside to hang out, ask yourself "Is this a friend or foe?" If she or he can't accept your decision to study, she or he is being selfish, and disrespecting your decision to study and the importance of school to you.

Peer pressure is real, and students are often striving for acceptance by peers in order to avoid being judged negatively. If you continue to hang out with those engaging in conversation, behavior, activities, etc. outside your values zone, it's only a matter of time before you'll succumb to theirs. Don't let fear of offending someone or rejection by those you want to be accepted by lead you to go along with things you perceive as wrong. Sometimes it's best to just walk away from a person or group too much in disharmony with your beliefs and preferences, especially when it's clear that they're not willing to change.

CHAPTER 11

Be Appropriately Assertive

There's a saying that goes, "What you permit, you teach." A large percentage of the stress that students experience comes from exposure to what others say and do to them, and many feel uncomfortable and ill-equipped to stand up for themselves in these undesirable situations. They tend to pushovers, chronic people-pleasers (as discussed in Chapter 3), and overly concerned with the consequences of standing up for themselves (e.g., hurting others' feelings, provoking anger, conflict or rejection). Appropriate assertiveness is needed. Without this, students are more vulnerable to the interpersonal stress that comes their way, which can detract from academic focus. You're worth and have the right to protect yourself from interpersonal harm.

Appropriate assertiveness isn't to be confused with selfishness; they're two different things. Selfishness is seeking to get what self wants without regard for the health of a relationship or the welfare of others. Appropriate assertiveness is endeavoring to facilitate healthy relationship functioning, and to protect yourself by saying and doing those things most likely to prevent, reduce, or eliminate the problematic things others may say or do to you. There's no guarantee that being appropriately assertive will improve things, but it's almost guaranteed that, if you say or do nothing, things won't improve but, in fact, may get worse.

Strategies to Develop Appropriate Assertiveness

Here are 13 strategies to develop appropriate assertiveness:

(1) Pray for what to say and do in challenging interpersonal situations, how to say and do it, and when to say and do it.

(2) Think of others as your equal because, if you feel inferior, it will foster non-assertiveness, and if you feel superior it will foster over-assertiveness (abrasiveness or aggressiveness); you're aiming for *appropriate* assertiveness.

(3) Learn to accept, like, and love yourself better, and to develop more self-respect (counseling may be required to achieve a healthy acceptance of yourself and greater self-respect) so you can genuinely and healthfully accept, like, love, and respect others. No one protects that which they don't value; if you don't like or value yourself and others, you'll mistreat both.

(4) Refrain from painting worst case scenarios when you think about letting someone know what you truly think or feel about her or him or a situation. If you think this way, you probably won't say or do anything about your predicament, and things will continue to be miserable.

(5) Don't remain silent or give in so easily when someone says or does something that bothers you—hold people accountable for their words and behavior. Try to speak up right then while the incident is still fresh in your mind, not days or weeks later. By then, she or he may not even remember what you're talking about and/or may dismiss your concerns because you've waited so long.

(6) Be more direct in what you think and feel, keeping in mind how you would like to be spoken to and treated if the situation was reversed. Be specific about your needs with others, but do so in a kind and tactful manner. It's okay to speak the truth without feeling guilty.

(7) Refrain from language such as, "You make me sick when you talk to me like that." Instead, wait until you're calm and use "I" language to address an issue or concern. For example, "I care about you and our relationship, but when you talk to me that way, I feel hurt." Or, "I know you mean well, but I feel put down when…" Or, "When you treat me like you just did, I feel anger towards you." Or "I feel unappreciated when you…" The point is, "I" communication is usually less threatening to the hearer, and may therefore minimize their responding defensively or angrily. However, give up the idea that you can *make* people change if you just say and do the right things. People change because they choose to, not just because you want them to.

(8) Watch your body language. If you're non-assertive, start making more direct eye contact with others. Stop hunching your shoulders, lowering your head, blinking repeatedly, or fidgeting every time someone says or does something that makes you feel uncomfortable. Talk more audibly so others won't have to strain to

hear you. Refrain from over-smiling and giggling; neither you nor your point will ever be taken seriously if accompanied with nervous laughter.

(9) If you're having major problems in a relationship, you might—when things are calm—say, "I care about you and our relationship and would like it to continue, so I need to talk with you about how I feel when you say or do… or we start…".

(10) Practice assertive behavior with a friend. You can also practice assertive behavior by closing your eyes, picturing a difficult situation, and imagining yourself dealing with the situation in an assertive manner. You might want to think of a challenging social situation, and rehearse a more assertive approach for when it next occurs. You can even record yourself to hear how you sound, since practice makes perfect.

(11) Let no one disrespect your time. Remember, "What you permit, you teach." Too many people will disrespect your time *if you let them*. For example, how many times have you scheduled an appointment with a healthcare professional for a specific time, and don't actually see her or him until much later, and she or he makes no apology. Patients are to blame in large part for this common phenomenon because most accept this practice.

But you're too busy to have your time abused like this. Ironically, if you're late for your healthcare appointment; you're often rescheduled for days or weeks later; sometimes, the recep-tionist can work you in for a later-in-the-day but even more rushed appointment. Next time you schedule an appointment with a healthcare provider, ask if you'll be seen by her or him *at the time given you*. If the receptionist can't answer in the affirmative, keep calling around. Emergencies do happen, but in most cases when you're sitting in a chair watching your precious time fly by, anxious that you'll be late for your next activity of the day, the healthcare provider has just overbooked—on your time.

(12) Take an assertiveness and/or public speaking class to develop your assertiveness and increase your comfort in speaking in front of others. Everyone struggles with negative self-conscious-ness from time-to-time, but the sooner one gets a handle on it the sooner one can enjoy life more.

(13) Purchase a self-help book, CD, DVD, etc. on asser-tiveness building. However, keep in mind that you're trying to build

appropriate assertiveness, and not inappropriate assertiveness, which seeks to get only what self wants, doesn't care about others' feelings or needs, and will run over people without a second thought. Plus, inappropriate assertiveness tends to leave others feeling victimized, often justifiably so.

CHAPTER 12

Improve Your Communication Skills

Good communication is the lifeblood of every relationship. Without it, relationships cannot reach their fullest potential and tend to be more distressing than a blessing, which can siphon attention, motivation, and energy from academic studies.

Here are 16 tips for successful communication:

(1) Pray to God that He help you improve your communication skills. Expect His full blessing here. He wants your communication with others to be such that He can use you maximally in ministering to others.

(2) Keep in mind that many relationship problems stem often from poor or inappropriate communication.

(3) Identify the areas in your communication that need improvement, and then pray to be able to take personal responsibility to do everything necessary to better *your* communication style. Also, encourage healthy communication in others by sharing these 16 tips with them, and voicing appreciation whenever you see them practiced.

(4) Talk *low* and *slow*, no matter what you discuss with others. It's highly unlikely that things will get out of hand when each communicates this way. However, if this tip fails, try sitting back-to-back to discuss the conflict, along with talking low and slow.

(5) Don't cut-off/interrupt others when they're speaking. Hear them out; you'll get your turn to do the same. Before a discussion, it's a good idea for individuals to pray for a fruitful discussion and agree to let each other speak without interruption.

(6) Maintain eye contact, and keep from engaging in other activities while people are speaking to you. Give them your undivided attention, just as you would like them to do for you.

(7) Be careful with your body language (don't turn your body away, roll your eyes, wave others off with your hand) when someone is speaking to you. Turn your body toward those with whom you're speaking, and keep your movements to a minimum.

(8) Listen for how others are feeling. If it isn't clear to you, ask them how they're feeling so you can be sure how the predicament is affecting them emotionally.

(9) Listen to *understand*, not to get your rebuttal (counter-argument) together. It's so very important that you listen to others to better understand their point of view, because what everybody wants when discussing an issue is for those involved to understand where they're coming from. When you're not clear about what someone is trying to say or get you to understand, ask questions.

(10) Don't dismiss, devalue, or be insensitive to another's view of a situation and/or feelings by saying such things as "I don't care what you think," or "You shouldn't feel like that." She or he has a right to their feelings and perceptions, even if you don't agree with them. Respect their thoughts and feelings. Show understanding, sensitivity, and empathy for their views by saying such things as, "I can tell that this whole situation is upsetting to you," or "I want you to feel better about this, what can I (or we) do to make it better?"

(11) Don't be demanding with others or lecture them with "shoulds" and "shouldn'ts." All this does is create a control/power struggle that makes matters worse or turns people off. Force is far from the best way to change others. Ideally, you want others to see their need to change and *choose* to do so. All you can do is be honest and to the point—in a tactful, loving, and respectful manner—and leave it to them to choose to change.

(12) Don't get caught up in blaming others and name-calling. When things get this heated, physical abuse or losing control in other ways is just a word or argument away. Someone needs to take a walk before violence erupts.

(13) Don't give loaded or generalized responses such as, "You don't know what you're talking about," "I know what your problem is," or "You never listen to me."

(14) When you're concerned or upset about something someone said or did to you, think through what you want to say and then honestly, tactfully, lovingly, and respectfully say it. Many find it helpful to write down what they want to say before sharing it with the person they're upset with to help them calm down and focus their concern. However, if the situation is so heated that you or the other person might erupt in words or behavior that will

make matters worse, then it's probably best to take a mutually agreed upon time-out. Cursing is always off-limits. Most arguing is pointless, and often leads to mutual resentment and greater stubbornness. The potential disadvantage of putting off the discussion is that it may not be as fresh in the minds of all involved when the predicament is finally discussed, and/or a build-up of resentment can lead to someone exploding later on. Exploding is far less likely if each person takes time to pray for the other and the situation before they resume the discussion.

(15) Regularly paraphrase or restate in your own words what others have shared with you; this shows that you heard them correctly. This is one of the most important and effective communication skills because it reduces misunderstandings, which often lead to conflict.

(16) Don't threaten to withdraw, withhold, or take something back from others because they're not acting the way you want; that's conditional love. Although challenging to do, practice unconditional love where you give and do your best for others *despite* their words or behavior, and be willing to apologize when you find yourself in the wrong.

CHAPTER 13

Avoid Use of Alcohol and Other Drugs, and Excessive Use of Technology and Television

Now, the third torpedo that sinks a student's academic life: an unhealthy relationship with some activity/thing—specifically, the use of alcohol and other drugs, and excessive use of technology and television.

There's probably no better way to destroy academic success (or one's life in general) than to use alcohol and other drugs and/or engage in the excessive (intemperate) use of technology and tele-vision. The use of alcohol and other drugs to cope with stress must be avoided. They *never* solve problems, but only create new ones. Alcohol is the most widely used depressant in the world. It reduces reasoning ability and negatively affects the brain and the liver, just to name a few organs that it damages. Here are some reasons students give for starting to drink: (1) to fit in/peer pressure; (2) to be "cool;" (3) because they believe everybody else is doing it; (4) to be popular; (5) to become more social; (6) to escape the stress and/or other difficult feelings from schoolwork, family, peers, or em-ployment; (7) because they believe college is where you party/have wild fun; (8) to get drunk; (9) to hurry the rite of passage into adult-hood; (10) to rebel against parental restrictions; (11) because alco-hol is accessible; and/or (12) out of curiosity.

What about caffeine, a stimulant? Caffeine is currently the world's most popular stimulant drug. With the proliferation and popularity of coffee houses, caffeine has become more accessible and more addictive than ever. Many students rely on the caffeine in coffee, "energy" drinks, soda pop, and pills to wake-up and to make it through the day, and the numbers of student users are swelling. If you habitually exceed 500 milligrams of caffeine a day, you're heading toward addiction. Withdrawal symptoms can in-clude headache, fatigue/sleepiness, anxiety, heart palpitations, irrit-ability, depression, difficulty concentrating, nausea and/or some-thing unique to you. Caffeine is a diuretic, so stimulates one to pee more and often which can cause dehydration. High doses of energy drinks can cause an irregular heartbeat and even heart attack.

Marijuana is the most popular illegal drug among students, and it adversely affects one's interest and motivation for school and other responsibilities. Many students use nicotine, especially in the form of cigarettes, to get through the stress of the day. Even chocolate—the aroma, the taste, the sugar, the caffeine in chocolate—can be quite addictive, and keep you coming back for more, especially if it's your favorite coping mechanism. You've probably read that chocolate has some health benefits. It does, but not the candy bar you may be thinking of. The chocolate investigated in these studies was pure dark chocolate *without* all the sugar, fat, and other additives that make it so appealing. These additives significantly diminish any health benefits.

What's addiction? An extreme craving or need for a substance or activity, continued use of a substance or activity despite negative life consequences, and inability to cut down or control use of a substance or activity. Often, what people are addicted to are the feelings that the substance or activity increases (excitement, pleasure, or some other desirable feeling) or reduces (tension, stress, or some other undesirable feeling) by engaging in the substance or activity, not the substance or activity per se. People addicted to a substance or activity no longer reach for the substance or activity, but the substance or activity seems to grab them.

As a person depends more and more on a substance or activity for the desirable feelings they produce or undesirable feelings they decrease, she or he can develop tolerance (the need for greater and greater amounts of the substance or activity to achieve the desired feeling or to prevent withdrawal). Withdrawal is mild to severe physical and/or psychoemotional pain and cravings for a substance or activity when there's a delay in the use of, or a reduction in the substance or activity.

It's very important to avoid excessive use of technology (e.g., the computer/Internet, Facebook, Twitter, LinkedIn, Tumblr, Hulu, Pinterest, Tumblr, Reddit, MySpace, YouTube, Craigslist, Backpage, movie websites, texting, tweeting, blogging, BuzzFeed, Instagram, Snap Chat, Vine, e-mail checking, playing video games/MMORPG (massively multiplayer online role playing game), smartphones, tablets, laptop computers), television, videos, and DVDs. Some people have a big "*app*etite." They're downloading *app*lications like mad and using them excessively. Many spend so much time scrolling through social media and texting that their fingers are ground to the bone! For multitudes, the *first* thing they think about when they wake up in the morning is technology, and then they compulsively reach for their technology to check for text messages, e-mail, or what's happening on social networking websites. And, all too often, the *last* thing they do before going to bed is check their technology again. (For many students, the last thing they *must* do just before class starts is check Instagram, text messages, Facebook, etc., and the first thing they *rush* to do the *moment* class ends is check their smartphones again.) The world is moving quickly from being centered on people to being centered on technology (a technocracy). Technology is eating away at our lives. There's nothing wrong with technology or television per se. They can be used responsibly for the good of self, others, and society, or be used irresponsibly for the not so good of self, others, and society.

Some Problems that Excessive Use of Technology and Television Can Cause

Here are ten problems associated with the excessive use of technology and television:

(1) They've become obsessions and taken over the lives of many. They're time-suckers and strip one of interest or desire to focus on *other* important responsibilities/activities of one's life such as personal devotions, witnessing, school work, household chores, exercising, getting needed rest, socializing with family and others, and being in the fresh air. How is it that the creator (of the technology) is controlled by the created (technology)? You should control technology and television; they shouldn't control you. Many will minimize or deny the severity of their technology or television use when confronted out of embarrassment, or to avoid having to accept that their technology or television use must be curtailed (if not given up). Several students have shared with me that technology or television wastes a lot of time and makes them lazy, *but they just can't stop.*

(2) One's thought-life often becomes preoccupied with Facebook, surfing the Internet, texting, tweeting, video games, tele-

vision, applications, etc., resulting in the crowding out of more productive thinking.

(3) They're often used as escapes from doing things that need to get done, such as studying. Things end up being put off until there's a *huge* backlog of things to be done, which creates even more stress because there's even more to do and even less time to do it in.

(4) Increases feelings of boredom (disinterest, discomfort, and inability to sit still and do nothing and/or find enjoyment in non-technology or non-television activities) and *intolerance* of it. *Reality* becomes boring. There's also a sense of greater and greater need for technology and television because of the stimulation they provide. For many, technology is no more than an adult pacifier. Many derive excitement or some other desirable feeling by living through the lives of the actors and actresses on television and the high stimulation of technology and most television programming. As a result, they experience strong urges to use technology and television for the desirable feelings they bring. Many students report that they've become so accustomed to being entertained by technology and television that they find studying *especially* boring.

(5) A smartphone is a daily interrupter, distracter, and concentration-breaker. A person can be studying, having a conversation, working, sleeping, or engaged in some other important activity, and when the smartphone rings, beeps, chirps, pings, or vibrates because of an incoming text message, tweet, e-mail, or phone call (which many can't ignore), she or he drops whatever she or he is doing to answer. Some are so hooked on their smartphones that they'll often grab it *believing* that they heard it sound or felt it vibrate only to find that it hadn't. Many fear being without their smartphone, and thus they take it with them wherever they go (e.g., to bed, the bathroom), obsessively check it, and never turn it off. Some live on their smartphones, and rarely look up. For many, texting has all but replaced regular face to face communication. Some have become so dependent on their smartphones that they've become *less* smart.

(6) Technology is isolating us and impairing social skills because most communication is now done via technology. Without regular practice, social skills weaken.

(7) The repeated interruptions from text messages, tweets,

e-mails, and phone calls take away from being relaxed in the here and now because one is reachable 24/7. Many end up anxious from either anticipating a call, text message, tweet, or e-mail, or anxious to make a call, text, tweet, or e-mail to someone. Some are startled when their smartphone sounds or vibrates.

(8) Television can damage self-worth and one's own sense of life-satisfaction because of the glamorous picture painted of celebrities and their lifestyle (which tends to be materialistic). Many long for the lifestyle of these actors or actresses, but can't achieve it, so they often end up feeling even more frustrated and dissatisfied with themselves and their lives. Some students report that they're so absorbed in television that their lives are *forgotten*. Television in general distorts one's view of reality.

(9) Television can increase selfishness and disrespect of others, reduce verbal and behavior self-control, and undermine one's ability to resist temptation because most television programming reeks of self-gratification, disrespect of others, and violence.

(10) They're hazardous to physical health (particularly television with its barrage of commercials about typically unhealthy food and beverages) because they lead to ingestion of more calories and breed inactivity, which increases weight gain. This weight gain opens the door for other health problems.

Strategies to Avoid Excessive Use of Technology and Television

Here are seven strategies to avoid excessive use of technology and television:

(1) Deny your denial that you excessively use technology and/or television. Be honest with yourself and admit that technology and/or television consumes way too much of your time.

(2) Pray for the willingness and power to commit to do whatever's necessary to break free of excessive use of technology and/or television. Overcoming technology and television addiction requires an inward determination sustained by prayer.

(3) Ask yourself, "What am I thinking and feeling just prior to diving into excessive use of technology or television?" About 99% of the time it's because you're thinking or feeling something negative or unpleasant such as boredom, stress, loneliness, empti-

ness, etc. that you're trying to escape from or reduce through the excessive use. Whatever negative feeling you're going through *will* pass if you wait it out. The point is—you don't have to reach for technology or television for relief.

(4) When the strong urge arises to escape a task that needs to get done through the use of technology or television, do the right thing in the vulnerable moment by praying for power to resist the urge. The intense desire to escape the task will soon subside, and you'll find yourself task-focused. Also, instead of giving in to the excessive use, go for a walk, do some push-ups, study, touch base with someone you haven't spoken to in some time—things good for you and not harmful.

(5) Limit the amount of time spent on technology and television. Schedule *increased* time in your weekly planner for responsibilities/activities such as personal devotions, witnessing, studying, exercising, getting needed rest, and *reduced* time for using technology or television.

(6) If you can't limit your use of technology and television, you'll have to cancel all Facebook, MySpace or Twitter accounts, disconnect your Internet service, dump your television, etc.

(7) If none of the above works, get professional help ASAP. (For some students, common sense and self-control hasn't sunk in yet, and so they may need professional assistance to develop in these areas.) You can't serve two masters: God and excessive use of technology or television. God will lose out every time.

Some questions to honestly answer and think about: (1) What's your favorite addiction? That is, what substance or activity do you find yourself continually overindulging in? (2) What are the ways in which you justify your addiction? (3) How much easier does it seem to do your addiction as time passes? (4) When are you going to wake up and realize that sooner or later, unless you overcome your addiction, it will destroy you, your life, and/or hurt those who care about you?

CHAPTER 14

Eat Regularly and Healthfully

Students are busy, having little time (it seems) to prepare a "real" meal. It's also a challenge to eat regularly and healthfully when family and friends are doing the opposite and/or are unsupportive of healthy eating habits. Nutritious food is, however, vital for good health and optimal functioning. That old saying, "Your health is your wealth," is true. Just ask anybody who has had to deal with an acute or chronic physical health problem.

The human body functions best on a simple diet of fruits (nature's candy), vegetables, whole grains, legumes (beans), and nuts. Reduce or eliminate saturated and trans fats (hydrogenated or partially hydrogenated oils), cholesterol laden products (meat, cheese, milk, margarine/butter, eggs), and beverages and foods loaded with sugar or salt. Stay away from fast food restaurants. The majority of the items they dish up only increase your weight, undermine good health, and reduce your energy level.

Trans fats are often used to deep-fry foods and can be found in many baked goods, margarine, and shortening. Trans fat is harmful to the heart because it lowers good cholesterol (HDL) and raises bad cholesterol (LDL).[9] Fast food is also chockfull of sodium (salt). Sodium is used as a preservative and seasoning. High levels of sodium exist in canned soups, frozen dinners, salad dressings, pancake mix, and cereals, and contributes to the development of hypertension, kidney problems, calcium loss, and stomach cancer. Salt alternatives include low-salt substitutes, lemon juice, and spices. Frequent eating of fast food or junk food can so pervert taste preferences that an aversion to healthy food can develop. Many don't taste *food* anymore, just the seasonings they put in it and on it.

School Food

Cafeteria food, and the items in the snack machines at many schools, are notoriously unhealthy, so you'll have to make some difficult choices. One choice is to take a proactive role to change the menu. Gather other students with similar healthy food interests and approach the cafeteria head and/or Student Services about your needs—in a kind, respectful and tactful manner. You can present your concerns in written and/or verbal form. For those of you paying tuition, and room and board that pay for campus expenses from soap to salaries, you have a right to voice your dietary preferences. You'd be surprised how the powers that be are responsive to a civil and organized student effort; without students, no educational institution could stay in business for very long.

The Best Way to Start Your Day

It's so very important to start each day with a *healthy* breakfast.[10,11,12] No one would intentionally take off for a long road trip without filling up the gas tank beforehand, but people will regularly take off for a long school or work day without filling up with a healthy breakfast. The fast food sausage biscuit with a cinnamon roll and humongous cup of coffee isn't the best fuel to start the day. When the gas tank is low in your car, have you ever put soda pop in? Do you use pancake syrup when the oil dipstick says you're down about half a quart? Have you used vegetable oil to bring the brake fluid level up to the full line? Of course not! Why? Because you know that these substances will damage your car so that it doesn't run properly. No matter how low any of these fluid levels in your car get, you would never consider putting anything in their reservoirs but what the car manual prescribes.

So why, when you've been running on empty all day—having skipped breakfast or eaten a poor nutritional breakfast—do you raid the drive-thru and order the least healthy food for your body? What are you saying to God and yourself when you take better care of the car you ride in than the body (the temple of the Holy Spirit) you reside in? *That you value and respect your car more than you do your body?*

The only reason our bodies don't break down as quickly as a car does when the wrong things are put in them is because the human body is wonderfully and fearfully made. However, if we abuse our bodies long enough, breakdown will occur. If you neglect your health, you're casting to the ground important wealth.

The student motto should be "Eat to live, don't live to eat." Your body is so worth it. Our food choices shouldn't be dictated solely by taste, but by nutritional value. Get in bed early enough to wake up early enough to prepare a healthy breakfast. You can prepare some of your breakfast the night before and set the table, put your fruit out, pour your cereal in a bowl, etc. Students who start the day with a nutritious breakfast perform better academically than those students who don't have breakfast regularly.[13,14]

Regularity in eating is essential. Eat your breakfast, lunch, and dinner around the same time each day, with at least 5 hours between meals.[15] Students who have little or no healthy breakfast or lunch typically eat too much unhealthy food late in the evening, and soon thereafter either go to bed or engage in some sedentary activity. Avoid this common practice at all costs. These calories from eating late go unburned and are stored in the body as fat;[16] this is a sure recipe for courting obesity.

Many students report not being hungry for breakfast in the morning. Some of the reasons behind this diminished appetite are: (1) a late last-night heavy meal being digested in the stomach; (2) anxiety and pressure from rushing to get to class or some other appointment; (3) waking up groggy from a poor night's sleep; and (4) not eating breakfast has become such a habit that the body has become accustomed to it and sends out little to no hunger signals. Many students report that there's simply not enough time to eat a sit-down breakfast. These issues can be resolved if you schedule time for breakfast in your weekly planner, and lighten or eliminate the evening meal. Lightening or eliminating dinner is a great natural way to manage weight. If you must eat something in the evening, try fruit salad or a salad topped with raw vegetables, sprouts (e.g., alfalfa, mung bean, broccoli, buckwheat) or tofu. Many students could probably get away with two meals a day—breakfast and a late lunch. Prepare a healthy lunch the night before to eat the next day, or eat lunch at a restaurant that serves healthy meals. Your biggest meal should be breakfast, and dinner the smallest.

If possible, reduce egg use or exclude them altogether. Eggs contain anywhere from 150-215 milligrams of cholesterol, depending on the size of the egg, and the RDA (recommended dietary allowance) is *less* than 300 milligrams of cholesterol a day. How many people do you know who eat only one egg at a meal? If you must consume eggs, consider egg substitutes, which typically are made up of the white part of the egg and contain no cholesterol. There's really no need to ingest dietary cholesterol because the human body (i.e., liver) produces sufficient amounts.

About Meat

Meat-eating is harmful to the body. Millions of pounds of meat have been recalled due to contamination by pathogens. Meat, including seafood, can be acid-forming, lacks fiber; it causes constipation, intestinal toxins, fatigue, and weakness. Most meat is full of saturated fat, cholesterol, excess protein, antibiotics, growth hormones, dirt, dust, fecal matter, urine, worms, maggot larvae, cancer viruses, bacteria such as salmonella, e-coli, and listeria[17,18,19] and dead blood—all of which is unhealthy. Meat is essentially seasoned dead animal tissue. Much of the refrigerated or canned meat and fish is infused with sodium nitrite to "preserve" it.[20] Think of this additive as an embalming agent to keep meat and fish from discoloring, rotting, and teeming with bacteria. Sodium nitrite can be toxic, and when combined with other chemicals in the body it forms carcinogens,[21] particularly the ones that cause gastric cancers.[22] We humans were originally designed as herbivores (plant eaters),[23] not carnivores (meat eaters).

You may say you need meat for the protein but the best source of protein for us, as herbivores, is plant-based: beans, grains, and vegetables.[24,25] Tofu (made from soybeans) is a versatile plant protein because it can be consumed in various dishes at breakfast, lunch, and dinner. Lentils are also protein-packed. Other good sources of protein include whole grains, dark green leafy vegetables, and potatoes.

What about fish for the omega-3 fatty acids? You can obtain omega-3 fatty acids from chia or flax seeds, or soymilk fortified with omega-3 fatty acids. Chia is also abundant in antioxidants, vitamins, minerals, protein, and fiber. Chia also doesn't go rancid when in oil form or crushed. Chia or flax seeds can be sprinkled on hot and cold cereals, salads, brown rice, any vegetable, or mixed in with a homemade smoothie or your favorite beverage. Chia, flax seed, and brewer's yeast also provide the ten essential amino acids. If you really want to do your body good, consider a *total* vegetarian, or vegan, diet.

Research shows that total vegetarians have lower cholesterol and body mass indexes (weight), less risk of contracting high blood pressure, Type 2 diabetes, prostate or colorectal cancer, or dying of heart disease than do those who eat red meat, poultry, fish, milk products, eggs, or other animal products.[26] A total vegetarian diet also provides more water, fiber, and nutrients than a meat-laden diet because of the plentiful amounts of fruits and vegetables consumed, and can prevent up to 97% of heart attacks.[27] Meat has zero fiber and is associated with higher rates of cancer and cardiovascular disease deaths.[28] The World Cancer Research Fund and American Institute for Cancer Research strongly recommend a reduction in meat intake to decrease cancer incidence.[29]

About Milk

Cow's milk is meant for calves, not humans.[30] Cow's milk is different from human milk; it contains four times more protein than human milk, and 82% casein compared to 20% casein in human milk.[31] A majority of the cows from which milk comes from have been given recombinant bovine growth hormones (rBGH) and antibiotics in order to increase their growth and keep down disease. Residue of these substances, as well as pesticide and fungal contaminants, have been found in the milk.[32]

What about calcium? You can obtain sufficient calcium from dark green leafy vegetables, tofu, soybeans and soy nuts, figs, and calcium-fortified soy, rice or almond milk. Soy products also reduce cholesterol, LDL levels, and risk of breast and colon cancer.[33]

About Soda Pop

Soft drinks. Why are they called "soft" when they're so hard on the body? It's difficult to resist those fountain drinks, especially when they come with free refills. Soda pop (liquid candy) isn't good for the body. It's carbonated, usually contains artificial colors and flavors, caffeine (in some products), and an all-time-favorite—sugar. The sugar in just about all non-diet soft drinks is either high fructose corn syrup (made from corn) or sucrose (made from sugar cane). Typically, high fructose corn syrup is used because it's sweeter and cheaper than sucrose.[34] A 12–ounce soft drink may contain from seven to twelve teaspoons of sugar,[35,36] and soda pop accounts for 21% of all the sugar ingested in the United States.[37] Sugar has no nutritional value; the only thing it has going for itself is that it tastes good, which unfortunately is what draws so many to it. Sugar contributes to tooth decay, obesity, personality changes and mood swings, the depletion of essential vitamins and minerals, and increases the risk of diabetes, heart disease, arthritis, and hypertension.[38]

Instead, try drinking organic 100% fruit juices diluted by half with water; this will reduce the natural sugar concentration and allow you to ingest more water. Please know, however, that the juice from fruit (and vegetables) was meant to be eaten with the "flesh" of the fruit (and vegetables) so that we can benefit from their fiber content.[39] Added sugar seems to be in everything; including jelly, ketchup, and peanut butter (yes, peanut butter!).

The next recommendation is tough because we're so used to doing just the opposite, but refrain from drinking beverages during meals; they only dilute the gastric juices and slow the digestive process. It's best to drink beverages (preferably water) between meals, and no later than 15 minutes before the next meal.[40] Drink to live, don't live to drink.

About Food Additives

There's hardly a processed food out there that doesn't have additives in it. While some additives are benign, most are not.[41,42,43] The additives are designed to make food look better, taste better, and last longer on the store and home shelf, but the long-term effects of these substances haven't been adequately studied.[44]

Here are some words of strong advice: *read the ingredients list on whatever you buy*. If you can't pronounce the ingredients on the list because they sound like something from chemistry class, leave it on the shelf. Also, remember that the amount of each ingredient is listed in descending order from most to least. For example, if you pick up a box of breakfast cereal and the ingredients list says "Sugar, artificial flavors, whole wheat," most of the product is made of sugar, with artificial flavors second, and wheat third. The front of the cereal box may say it's a "nutritious" whole wheat cereal, but the ingredients list says otherwise.

Let's look at some additives to avoid.

Flavorings. Why would any food need added flavorings unless it doesn't taste good to begin with? If you read "artificially-flavored" on the ingredients list, it means that whatever was used to flavor the product is artificial, something cooked up in a lab that is inferior in quality and much less expensive than the real thing. One flavor enhancer, Monosodium Glutamate (MSG), has no flavor of its own but enhances other flavors and imparts a savory taste.[45] It can be found in canned soups, frozen dinners, instant noodles and most fast foods, and can cause faintness, tremors, muscle weakness, and headaches in *sensitive* individuals.[46] Watch out for the preservatives BHA and BHT. They can be found in candy, chewing gum, and breakfast cereals, and have been found to affect liver and kidney functioning and trigger allergic reactions.[47] Another preservative, sodium benzoate, has been linked to hyperactivity in children and can react with added vitamin C to make benzene—a cancer causing substance.[48] Although many beverages containing sodium benzoate and added vitamin C have been reformulated to meet FDA safety standards, it's still not clear how much benzene consumers could be exposed to from beverages.[49]

Sulfites. These are freshness enhancers sprayed on fruits and vegetables, and used in dried fruits, beer, and wine. Some of the names for these sulfites are metabisulfite, sodium sulfite, and sulfur dioxide. Asthmatics and allergy sufferers should avoid sulfites.[50]

Artificial coloring. You've seen them in the ingredients list on many packages (e.g., FD&C Red No. 3 or 40). They can be found in fruit-flavored Jell-O and popsicles, ice cream, soft drinks, puddings, and colored candies, and have been linked to asthma, runny eyes and noses, blurred vision, and hyperactivity in children.[51,52] Other harmful additives include propylene glycol, tannin, EDTA, and animal mono- and diglycerides.[53]

The Importance of Water and Fiber

Drink at least 6-8 cups of water a day, depending upon your degree of fluid loss, outside temperature, body weight, etc. Your skin is the largest excretory organ of the body.[54] That's why we ought to bathe regularly, to wash off the impurities on the skin that can create quite a smell and cause illness. If you shower or bathe the outside of your body regularly with water, why not use the same fluid for the inside of your body as well. Coffee, soda pop, or milk can no more cleanse the outside of your body than it can the inside. The human body is mostly made up of water and, just as the outside requires water to be cleansed and refreshed, so does the inside need this precious fluid to flush and revitalize your system, and maintain optimal body functioning. Lack of sufficient amounts of water dehydrates cells, tissues, and fluids in the body, and thickens the blood which increases risk of stroke and heart disease.[55]

Are you drinking enough water? Sometimes tiredness, headaches, and low energy can be attributed to insufficient water. If your urine is very yellow to dark gold and strong smelling, you're probably not drinking enough water. Ideally, your urine should be pale with little odor.[56] However, if you're taking vitamins or medications, or eating certain vegetables or fruits, your urine will probably be less than clear and have an odor.

You can also tell if you're not getting enough water or fiber if your bowel movement is infrequent (i.e., 3 or fewer a week) and uncomfortable, if not painful. If your stool is *often* pellet-like, has a consistently very foul smell, sinks quickly, and doesn't at least partially disintegrate upon flushing, you probably need more water and fiber in your diet. Fiber helps reduce cholesterol and triglycerides, and provides better glucose control for diabetics and non-diabetics.[57] Some great sources of fiber include beans, brown rice, oatmeal, wheat bulgur, avocado, berries (preferably organic to avoid unhealthy chemicals), and Kashi GOLEAN and Uncle Sam cereals.

Habits Associated with Poor Health

It's no secret that many students are tired, sickly, broken down, going back and forth to the doctor's office, taking prescription and over the counter medications day-in and day-out, or are unhappy with what they see in the full-length mirror. Being overweight to obese is epidemic in the United States and many other industrialized countries. Just look around (or, perhaps, *down?*). It doesn't have to be that way; you *can* gain greater control over your physical health. Just as the laws of gravity apply to everyone (whether one believes them or not), the laws of health apply to everyone as well (whether one believes them or not). It's so very important to practice lifestyle habits that support good health, because lifestyle is strongly associated with health and mortality.[58] If you don't engage regularly in health-promoting practices, your health can become so poor that you may start longing for death to put you out of your misery. Students tend to take their health for granted. However, this attitude must change if students want to live to a ripe old age.

Here's a list of eight habits associated with poor health:

(1) Little or no breakfast.

(2) Eating heavy evening meals.

(3) Moderate to high intake of refined foods.

(4) Moderate to high intake of saturated and trans fats and cholesterol (e.g., milk, cheese, eggs, ice cream, cookies).

(5) Little or no intake of fresh fruits and vegetables.

(6) Eating snack/junk food or processed food.[59]

(7) Refusal to get a regular physical exam or see a health care provider when something just doesn't seem to be going right with your body (usually from fear that something wrong will be discovered).

(8) Nonchalance regarding gaining health knowledge, resulting in not knowing what things you should and shouldn't do to reduce health problems.

Habits Associated with Good Health

Here's a list of ten habits associated with good health:

(1) Maintaining an ideal weight (or body mass index).

(2) Eating breakfast regularly.

(3) No snacking.

(4) Eight hours of sleep each night.

(5) Exercising regularly.

(6) Abstinence from alcohol or other drugs (including nicotine).[60]

(7) Limited, in-control use of technology and television.

(8) A sense of humor.

(9) A strong social support network.

(10) A vibrant spirituality (e.g., strong prayer life, study of the Bible and Spirit of Prophecy, church attendance and participation, witnessing).

Don't attempt too big a change in your habits or lifestyle right away; otherwise shock might kick in leading to flight back to the old ways. Take it a step at a time; instead of going cold turkey with fast food, cut back little by little until you're completely off of it. Some can stop cold turkey. These guidelines aren't designed to take the fun out of life, but to enable longer life to have fun. The goal isn't to achieve ideal health overnight, but to get there and stay there at a pace that works for you.

About Eating and Body Image Disorders

Some students suffer from eating disorders (severe disturbances in eating behavior) which can compound the stress in their life. When it comes to food, it's about when you eat, what you eat, how much you eat, how often you eat, and why you eat. Six disorders stand out among students:

(1) Bulimia Nervosa (episodes of binge eating with purging). Binge eating is extreme overeating. Binge eaters usually feel a loss of control while binge eating. The binge can be triggered by stress, relationship conflicts, hypersensitivity to social interactions, low self-worth, depression, intense hunger, or negative feelings about one's general appearance. The foods consumed can vary, but are usually sweet, high-calorie, and tasty (ice cream, cookies, or candies). Purging is effort to prevent weight gain through self-induced vomiting, or taking laxatives (to speed the passage of food through the digestive system so that less of it is absorbed by the body) or diuretics (to expel water weight). They also engage in fasting or excessive exercise to reduce weight. This disorder mostly affects females, and often occurs in secret because of shame. Those with this disorder are usually of normal weight or overweight. They possess ambivalent to negative feelings about their weight and shape, and seem to have a love-hate relationship with food.

(2) Binge Eating Disorder (repeated episodes of extreme overeating *without* purging). These individuals are usually overweight or obese, feel out of control when they eat, eat faster than others, and will often eat alone out of embarrassment should someone see how much they're eating. They may not even be hungry when they binge. The binges are usually triggered by stress, anxiety, depression, boredom, or some other undesirable emotion. Without

treatment, those with this disorder can develop Type 2 diabetes, hypertension, and cardiovascular disease.

(3) Emotional eating (eating comfort or preferred foods to feel better or not so bad because eating them is inherently enjoyable). Emotional eaters are often *not* even hungry, but eat these comfort foods in order to reduce stress, boredom, anxiety, depression, or other feelings related to low self-worth, relationship problems, family conflicts, school demands, work issues, financial problems, etc. This can lead to addiction to these comfort foods and increased weight gain which makes things worse because the person dislikes what she or he sees in the mirror and feels like she or he has lost control of another area of their life.

(4) Anorexia Nervosa (an intense, almost phobic fear of becoming fat, a distorted body image, and persistent behavior that interferes with weight gain). This disorder typically afflicts females, and starts during adolescence or young adulthood. Many of these females have bought into the media's depiction of "thin is in," and starve themselves through dieting or excessive restriction of food intake to achieve this irrational ideal. Although these females eat very little, they think about food often. Some become obsessed with exercise to keep their weight down. Those with Anorexia Nervosa often engage in binge-eating (with purging), lie about how much they're eating, and hide food. Although their weight drops dramatically, and family members and friends express significant concern over their emaciation, anorexics *still* believe that they're too fat, and continue to compulsively and uncontrollably limit food intake, and minimize or deny the seriousness of their condition.

Be careful of the media, especially television and magazines. They put pressure on females to look a certain way (thin, tanned, and big-bosomed). There's growing pressure on males to look a certain way as well (tall, tanned, and muscular), but it'll likely never rise to the level placed on females. The body images that the media hold up are typically outside the norm for both genders and can cause insecurities, low self-worth, and fears of rejection relative to body image if not lived up too. By the way, beauty or attractiveness comes in *all* shapes, sizes, and colors. The media will probably never change in featuring unrealistic standards of beauty, so *don't* let it turn you against yourself!

Other causes of Anorexia Nervosa include peer pressure,

criticism about one's weight from inside and/or outside the family, chronic family problems, stressful life events, constantly comparing one's body to others, perfectionism, wanting to attract the opposite sex, a desire to excel in sports and other activities that typically require low weight (e.g., gymnastics, running, ballet, modeling), fears of sexual maturity, or neurotransmitter problems. Anorexia Nervosa is a very serious disorder that often requires intensive outpatient treatment, if not hospitalization.

(5) Body Dysmorphic Disorder (obsessive negative concern or preoccupation with a particular part of one's body). This disorder afflicts both females and males, and can range from excessive negative concern and insecurities about the appearance of one's hair, eyes, facial complexion, nose, lips, teeth, and chin to the shape and size of one's chest, stomach, hips, thighs, buttocks, or legs. These individuals feel flawed physically and painfully self-conscious about their flaws, which leads to significant discomfort around others, social withdrawal, dramatic efforts to correct the flaws, or suicidal thoughts in severe cases.

(6) Obesity (a condition where an individual is overweight by 20% or more). A person whose diet is high in red meat, sugary desserts, high-fat foods, and highly refined grains is asking for weight gain and major health problems. As mentioned earlier, obesity is a major health problem in America, and many industrialized countries, and increases risk for hypertension, Type 2 diabetes, heart disease, stroke, osteoarthritis, sleep apnea, and colon cancer. The primary causes of obesity are lifestyle negligence (not eating right, drinking right, and lack of exercise), Binge Eating Disorder (discussed above), and/or emotional eating (discussed above).

Now the *primary* motivation to lose weight should be for maintenance of *health*, and *not* physical appearance reasons. Why? Because if your drive to lose weight is mainly to *look better*, you'll never be satisfied; there'll always be somebody who looks better to you, and this may discourage weight-loss efforts, or lead to endless dissatisfying efforts to achieve an unreachable ideal.

These eating and body image disorders above are best addressed by contacting your local mental health center, which can put you in touch with mental health professionals, registered dieticians, and physicians with expertise in these areas. These disorders can be beat with prayer and professional help.

CHAPTER 15

Regularly Exercise

Regularly engage in exercise that involves stretching to improve flexibility, cardiovascular effort (e.g., running, cycling, swimming, racquetball) to enhance heart health, and muscle resistance (e.g., weight training, pushups, isometrics) to increase strength at least three times a week for 50 minutes. If you can't pull off 50 minutes three times a week, do whatever amount you can at least three times a week. *Some* exercise is better than none at all. It's best to exercise first thing in the morning because it boosts your metabolism (the rate at which your body burns calories), helps you to feel more energized, and provides a feeling of accomplishment that you're doing something good about your health. Moderate exercise is one the most effective buffers for stress, and boosts the immune system's ability to fight off colds and other illnesses.[61,62] If you get sick from lifestyle negligence (not eating right, drinking right, and lack of exercise), you'll be unable to function at your best at school, work, home, or any responsibility. A recently completed 21-year study found that running slows the aging process, reduces rates of disability, and extends the life span.[63] Exercise is best done outside in the fresh air[64] (your lungs and other organs will love you for this). Don't let *anything* or *anybody* prevent you from exercising regularly. Incorporate time in your weekly planner for exercise.

Exercise has several benefits (all helpful to students) worth mentioning:

(1) Relieves stress, tension, and worry.
(2) Increases energy.
(3) Alters levels of neurotransmitters so that mood is improved.
(4) Increases alertness.
(5) Increases general self-confidence.
(6) Improves immune system functioning.
(7) Burns calories.
(8) Improves endurance.[65]

Note these risky exercise elements to avoid:

(1) Neglecting to get a physical examination before embarking on an exercise program.
(2) Lack of preparation.
(3) Exercising too intensely too often.
(4) Imbalance between training and recovery.
(5) Exercising in hot weather.
(6) Habitual inactivity.[66]

With prayer to stick with a sound exercise program and a proper diet, you'll not only improve your health and feel and look better, but will be primed for greater academic success. Don't overdo it with your exercise plan or discouragement can set in leading you to give it up.

CHAPTER 16

Get Good Sleep

One of the most common complaints I hear from students is that they're not getting enough sleep. Many are sleep deprived because of their too busy lifestyle. Sleep allows the body and brain to rest and rejuvenate itself after a day of dealing with stress, pressure, and demands.[67,68] Sleep also permits the brain to organize memories and cleanse itself of metabolic toxins, the immune system to rebuild itself, and for growth and development to occur (human growth hormone is made while asleep). Sleep also stabilizes mood and consequent social behavior. Most people need at least 8 hours of sleep a night.

Poor sleep is damaging in multiple ways. It causes sleepiness, decreases resistance to stress, impairs judgment, diminishes interest, energy, and motivation for various responsibilities, and undermines concentration and memory ability, causing performance and academic success to go down the drain. Additionally, sleep deprivation increases impatience, irritability, and anger, which adversely affects your relationships.

Some students suffer from insomnia (difficulty falling or remaining asleep throughout the night) secondary to worrying in bed about school, finances, relationships, etc. One effective way to deal with insomnia is to keep a notepad and pen or voice recorder nearby (as discussed in Chapter 6) and write down or voice record the concerns that pop up while trying to get to sleep, as a reminder of what to tackle the next day and so your mind can be clear to go to sleep. Little if any problem-solving occurs while trying to sleep anyway. Some have trouble getting to sleep because their bodies are still wired from all the caffeine and/or sugar consumed throughout the day. Going to bed soon after watching emotionally charged TV programs, DVDs, or videos, or listening to rousing music can keep you awake because of all the thoughts racing through your head and all the adrenalin in your system caused by what you saw and heard. Still others have difficulty getting or staying asleep because they went to bed too soon after eating a heavy evening meal. Your stomach should be empty when you go to bed.

Sometimes insomnia can be a symptom of an underlying psychological (e.g., anxiety disorder, hypomania) or medical disorder (e.g., hyperthyroidism, hyperglycemia), so discuss any chronic sleep problems with a physician. It's a good idea to have a bedtime routine (one or two relaxing things you consistently do prior to getting in the bed) to signal your mind and body that it's time to unwind/get ready to sleep. The most efficient sleep occurs between 9:00 p.m. and 12 midnight, [69] so the earlier to bed the better.

CHAPTER 17

Know and Respect Your Limits

When you know that you can't take on any more, and someone asks you to take on still more, just politely say something like, "No thank you, my work plate is already quite full." If you're involved in too much, less time and energy is available for school. No matter how much someone begs you to take on a task or claims that you're the *only* one who can do the job, resist giving in if you know you'll be overextending yourself. Don't let the ego rush of being needed drive you to agree to another responsibility when you know that you're already juggling too much. Also, try not to let people-pleasing tendencies, guilt, unawareness that helping others *doesn't* mean neglecting yourself, or difficulty being assertive lead you to take on more than you can handle.

As a general rule, when it comes to workload, you're obligated to do only your part or fair share, not anyone else's part or an unreasonable share. Compromise whenever possible, but never to the point where you neglect yourself, burnout, end up ineffective, or trample on your values. Get out if the cost of staying is greater than the cost of leaving, if there's *no* change in sight, and the Lord says move on. This applies to a relationship, job, extracurricular activity, anything that's taking a toll on you. Seek God in prayer for help in knowing and respecting your limits.

CHAPTER 18

Make Time to Relax

Don't take life so seriously. Give yourself permission to regularly take time to have wholesome fun and relax. Try not to get caught up in the belief that, if you're not busy doing something, then you're wasting time. School should no more be all play and no work than all work and no play. All work and no play can lead to resentment toward studying and to reduced academic success; all play and no work can lead to guilt over play and reduced enjoyment of recreational activities. A balance must be struck between the two. Remember that life isn't a sprint, but a marathon, so pace yourself. Do your best in trying to manage your numerous responsibilities; however, if it's not working, you'll need to cut some responsibilities out or reduce the amount of time spent on them. You shouldn't feel like a hamster in a wheel, just running and running, but not getting anywhere.

Because students are busy, it's important for them to spend at least 15 minutes or more a day being still and, basically, doing nothing. If sitting still, doing nothing, is difficult, you've bought into the lie that you're wasting time because you're not doing something worthwhile. You *are* doing something worthwhile: you're taking care of yourself by taking a break. We all need a break on a regular basis to recharge and rejuvenate. If being still and doing nothing is hard for you, start with something like listening to soft music, taking a warm bath, or getting a massage. (Massage is very effective in reducing muscle tension and stress, inducing relaxation.[70]) Then, make the move to sitting still, doing nothing, and meditating. Meditation facilitates a state of deep relaxation and physiological changes beneficial to brain wave activity, heart rate, and cortisol secretion.[71,72] Meditating on God's love, nature's beauty, and all things true, noble, just, pure, lovely, and good can go a long way to cultivate a calmness you'll want to experience continually.

You often hear people say "Don't lose your temper," but that's exactly what people need to do: lose their temper so that others aren't victims of it. Poor coping with stress can put you on edge in a major way, so watch that temper! A temper can lead to impatience, irritability, anger, hostility, or explosiveness in severe cases —especially when somebody says or does something you don't like, doesn't think or do as you would like, or when things don't go the way you think they should. Remember, people can't *make* you angry; they can only say or do things that they think will get you angry or hurt you. A lot of the time people have no *intention* of provoking you; they're just expressing how they think and feel— though it comes across rather roughly. Also, you could be angry or hurt because you misunderstood or incorrectly read into what someone said or did. Check your perception out before reacting. Letting someone "have it" when you believe she or he intentionally "made" you angry or hurt you doesn't solve the problem; it only escalates it. If we all had less pride and more humility, we wouldn't be so sensitive and overreact to the things said or done to us.

Don't let anybody push your "hot buttons." If you do, you're just giving her or him power over you—to negatively affect you. She or he may use that power every chance possible.

The stress of being short-fused raises adrenalin, cortisol, epinephrine, homocysteine, C-reactive protein, and LDL cholesterol levels.[73] These physiological anomalies can further erode your ability to handle stress, which can contribute to high blood pressure, headaches, migraines, strokes, ulcers, sleep disorders, heart disease and heart attacks, and reduced immune system functioning.[74] Brain chemistry can be altered, which can increase suspiciousness, distrust, and social withdrawal. An explosive temper can push people away from you, and warrants a counselor's assistance. One excellent source of help for anger is anything by W. Doyle Gentry, Ph.D., author of numerous books on anger management.

Also, stay out of the business of trying to control others. It doesn't work, or it's too much work. You can't *make* anyone be what you want her or him to be, or what you think she or he ought to be. You don't have to win others over to your point of view; just practice what you know to be right, and allow others their right to choose what they believe. If two people can't agree to disagree, or their beliefs are just too disparate to reconcile, then the relationship probably won't work. Next time you believe someone did you wrong, do them right. You might be surprised how much better you and the other person feels, and the relationship may improve.

CHAPTER 19

Avoid Worry or Catastrophizing

Avoid worry or catastrophizing. Stay in the here and now. Worrying is fretting over all the things that could go wrong with self, a situation, or a relationship. It has been said that "Worrying is like a rocking chair: it gives you something to do but you don't get anywhere." Worrying helps in no way, so why do it? Catastrophizing is expecting the worst to happen at any moment to self, in a situation, or in a relationship. Think of catastrophizing as worrying on steroids, and it can breed so much stress, tension, and anxiety that studying becomes almost impossible. If you worry, and everything turns out fine, you've suffered emotionally for nothing.

Strategies to Avoid Worry and Catastrophizing

Here are five strategies to avoid worry and catastrophizing:

(1) Launch into *prayer* about your concerns the moment they try to take over your thinking. This is a most effective antidote for worry and catastrophizing.

(2) Confront the source of your worry or catastrophizing directly—don't ignore or deny it (it won't go away, and typically gets worse). Instead, apply these five problem solving steps: (a) identify what the stress is (e.g., I can't pay all my bills); (b) break the stress down (e.g., I have more bills/debt than income to pay them, I tend to buy on impulse, most of my purchases are for wants and not needs, I use my credit cards way too much); (c) explore possible strategies to cope with the stress (e.g., develop a budget, wait 24 or more hours before any major purchase, prioritize needs over wants, make purchases with cash or a debit card only, cut up all credit cards except one for emergencies only, talk to a debt counselor); (d) select one or two of the strategies and try them out (e.g., use only my debit card for purchases and cut up all but one credit card—which is for emergencies only); and (e) evaluate the effectiveness or outcome of the strategy(ies) you've tried. If the effectiveness or outcome isn't desirable (e.g., doesn't improve your

being able to pay bills/reduce debt), go back to the fourth step (d) and give another strategy a try (e.g., make an appointment with a debt counselor).

(3) Stop negative self-talk immediately: any negative or counterproductive thoughts about self, a situation, or a relationship. It undermines hope that things can change and discourages effort to overcome obstacles.

(4) Refrain from complaining about self, a situation, a relationship, or life in general; it only feeds fear, discouragement, and desperation. It's much more constructive to maintain an optimistic attitude about stress by asking the question: "What can I learn about myself and life from this predicament or relationship so I can prevent it from happening in the future or cope with it better next time?" If you're tired of the teacher (stress), then learn the lesson (how to cope) and pass the test so the teacher doesn't have to keep testing you until you get it.

(5) Be clear about what you can and can't control so you don't stress over things you can do little, if anything, about.

Here are some ways of thinking or beliefs I've observed in students that need changing to minimize worrying and catastrophizing: (1) I must be perfect—in how I look, act, talk, everything (Focus on character development instead); (2) people should be like me—think like me, feel like me, have preferences like me, respond like me, etc.; (3) you can't trust anyone, so I won't let anyone get close; (4) because I'm a nice person people should treat me right; (5) I must get an "A" (You don't *need* "As;" just do the *best* you can, and focus on ALS rather than GPA); (6) I'm dumb because I failed the exam (No, you probably just need to adjust your preparation strategy, or maybe it was a difficult exam that many did poorly on); (7) I must have nice things to be successful and happy (Materialism never brings *lasting* happiness); (8) life should be fair (Not in *this* life); (9) it's better to avoid problems than confront them, (10) you owe me—for all I've done for you and/or put up with about you; (11) I can't be happy unless things go *my* way (If everybody believed this way, there'd *always* be many unhappy people); and (12) I shouldn't have to change (Oh yes you do; if you're not changing or growing for the better, you're limiting your potential). Add your *own* ways of thinking or beliefs and then pray for power to overcome them so that worrying and catastrophizing can be minimized.

CHAPTER 20

Manage Your Finances

A critical area students must be attentive to is finances. Some students are well-off, but most are on meager funds. Now is the time to distinguish between needs and wants. Needs are necessary for your survival, wants aren't. It's okay to want nice things, as long as your wants don't rise to the level of materialism or lead to the neglect of taking care of needs. Too many students want what they want *now*, in terms of "things," without regard for the reality of their financial situation. Much of life is about timing—the ideal time to say or do certain things. Trying to obtain wants (e.g., an expensive car, a sprawling place to live, the latest fashions and technology), while pursuing a degree is often not ideal timing. And that's because making money ends up taking priority over school. Once a student can distinguish between needs and wants, and minimize striving for wants, stress decreases, and contentment abounds.

Don't overspend. You can enjoy your possessions so much more when purchased at the right time without struggling to pay off the debt. However, keep in mind that lasting happiness and material possessions don't mix. Things break down, wear out, and go out of fashion. Then, what happens to your happiness?

Debt is a major stressor. When you charge your credit card(s) to the hilt, the bank tacks on all the interest up front, and all the payments you make go *first* to pay off the interest *before* any starts going to pay off the principle (or what you charged up). By the time you finish paying off the debt, you'll have paid back much more than you actually borrowed.

If you're currently in debt, here are five surefire strategies to get out of debt and stay out of debt: (1) make a list of all the debt that you have so that you can see how much you owe, (2) deny your denial that you have a problem with money, and commit to do whatever's necessary to become debt-free—prayer will likely be required to achieve this second step as well as the remaining three, (3) don't take on anymore debt (stop charging), (4) make a financial lifestyle change—cut out what you don't need, prioritize needs over wants, and change your spending habits (e.g., no impulse buying, no emotional buying, no trying to keep up with what other students are buying, no materialism), and (5) prioritize your debt from the smallest to the largest, and pay off the smallest debts first. As these smaller debts are paid off, don't take the payments used to retire this debt and splurge; apply the payments to your larger debts.

Be a good steward of the funds given to you by God by, first, returning a regular and honest tithe (10% of your gross income) and offering (based on how much you want to say thank you to God for *all* the blessings He provides). God can enable you to do more with what you have left over *after* tithes and offerings than if you chose to do your own thing with it all.

Also, consider setting aside at least $20.00 or more a month to go into a benevolent fund you draw from to discretely help others in need, and another $30.00 or more monthly for personal emergencies.

CHAPTER 21

Talk to a Counselor When Indicated

Many students bring to school a wide variety of stressful challenges: low self-worth, anxiety and mood disorders, codependency, addictions, learning disorders, etc. The factors that underlie these challenges can include family of origin dynamics, emotional trauma, genetic inheritance, or other complex factors. These stressful challenges can fuel academic underachievement and dissatisfaction.

Whatever the cause of your particular struggle(s), put aside any fears about counseling and get the help you need. Make an appointment with a counselor (either at your school or in the community). Why keep suffering in silence when help is available? The counselor will help you develop solutions to your difficulties.

Every student can benefit from "a check up from the neck up" regarding stress relative to:

(1) Oneself (identity development, self-worth issues, holding fast to sound values and morals, managing one's self and life).

(2) School (being away from home—the familiar—and adjusting to living at school—the unfamiliar, academic pressure, deciding on a major and career).

(3) Significant others (developing and maintaining healthy primary relationships, handling conflicts and breakups with boyfriends and girlfriends).

(4) Peers (feeling accepted, a part of and/or belonging to a support network, peer pressure).

(5) Family (unresolved issues with parents, siblings, relatives).

(6) Work (being dependable, dealing with coworkers, supervisors, customers)

(7) Life in general.

(8) Anything of major concern to you.

Here are seven things to look for in an effective counselor:

(1) Licensed. However, it's okay to see a counselor in training because she or he is always under the supervision of

a licensed or certified mental health professional.

(2) Has training and/or experience in the area you're having difficulty in.

(3) Listens attentively and gives regular encouragement and feedback.

(4) Is sensitive to gender, racial, cultural, religious or any other unique demographics. It's especially important that your counselor is comfortable praying with you, praying for you, and allowing you to pray.

(5) Has user-friendly or flexible hours.

(6) Will consider modifying their fee if you're having legitimate financial challenges or problems.

(7) Is mentally stable themselves.

Ideally, you want to interview a potential counselor over the phone to gain a sense of where she or he stands in these areas. However, you likely won't be able to determine where the potential counselor stands relative to the third and seventh questions until you actually sit down with her or him.

If the counselor should recommend an evaluation for medicine by a psychiatrist (or other qualified health professional), follow through. Sometimes stressful challenges can be severe, or have their origin in neurotransmitter anomalies, so that significant or meaningful improvement can occur only with the help of medicine. Heart disease or diabetes isn't treated by a physician talking to the cardiovascular system or pancreas, telling them to perform as they should. Rather, they're treated by the physician who prescribes medicine (along with a lifestyle change) designed to address the problem. In the same way, some psycho-emotional problems are best managed with a psychotropic (medicine for the brain) along with a lifestyle change. In other words, if the problem is organic in nature, talking (counseling) alone probably won't solve it.

There are also some natural mental health remedies that work as well as some psychotropics—drugs that affect one's mental state. For alternative mental health see alternativementalhealth.com, for alternative medicine see nccih.nih.gov, naturalmedicine.com, naturalmedicinescomprehensivedatabase, wholehealthmd.com, gbhealthwatch.com, makinghealthez.com, and DrMikeLara.com, and for information on the quality of supplements and foods see consumerlab.com and examine.com). Natural mental health remedies have the advantage of fewer, if any, side effects, but the disadvantage of possibly not being potent enough if a person's mental health condition is severe. Naturopathic Doctors (N.D.) are known to be versed in alternative treatments and are a good resource to pursue if you're looking for more natural treatment strategies. Be sure to share any alternative treatments with your M.D. or D.O. (Doctor of Osteopathy) if you're working with one; some are familiar and open to alternative treatments.

In addition, a good cry from time-to-time is okay, as it helps purge the heart of hurt. Writing your stressful experiences in a journal can also relieve stress and encourage healing. If you're uncomfortable about approaching a counselor for help, try talking initially to your closest peer and/or trusted adult in your social support network, or join or start a support group relative to the stress in your life. Just don't do *nothing* about your problems; help and relief are available.

CHAPTER 22

Draw on Spiritual Beliefs and Practices 24/7

There's no denying it. We're not alone. There's a God Who is all-powerful, all-knowing and present everywhere at the same time, and He loves all of us. He created you and me, and sent His Son Jesus Christ to pay the penalty for your sin and mine—His death as a substitute for ours. He died, and then rose from the grave and intercedes before God the Father for all those who believe in Him, seek forgiveness and deliverance from sin, and desire to do His will.

God wants only the best for you. Spiritual maturity (being like Jesus Christ) is a must in order to better handle stress. This starts with conversion (turning from living for self to living for God). Next comes the sanctification process (becoming more and more like Jesus Christ), which takes place over a lifetime. A person has to die daily to self (change the focus from what *I* want, to what *God* wants). The more solid a person's spirituality as reflected in obedience to Jesus, not out of fear or legalism (attempting to earn favor or salvation with God through doing good things), but out of love for Him because of His love for us—the better her or his ability to cope with the challenges of life. One's spirituality is also reflected by a significant prayer-life, regular Bible study, fellowship with others who want to be like Jesus, serving those in need, and witnessing about Him.

Find a church to worship in with others who want to be like Jesus Christ. Pray, study God's Word, meditate on Him, and pray to Him, and see for yourself how a personal relationship with Him can supply you with a sense of purpose, fulfillment, peace, and joy you never thought possible.

Many continue in a path that seems right to them because they haven't been informed of a better way. Jesus Christ is the Better Way. It's often been said that, "Man's disappointments are God's appointments." God can use stressful predicaments to mature your Christ-likeness (bring you further along in the sanctification process), so that you experience peace within despite chaos without. Therefore, view stressful circumstances as growth-promoting opportunities rather than as unwanted obstacles. This perspective helps reduce feeling stressed, overwhelmed, and/or discouraged, and facilitates academic success.

The research is clear: spiritual practices such as prayer and meditation on God's Word are effective strategies in building moral stamina and mitigating the deleterious effects of stress.[75,76] *Prayer might not change things for you, but you for things.* That is, prayer can help you to better deal with challenges when they occur (e.g., God might not move the mountain, but give you the strength to climb). If you're already spiritually oriented, earnestly draw on spiritual beliefs and practices to gain strength and confidence to cope with stress. If there's a chaplain or church pastor on your campus, consider confiding in her or him. If she or he can only help you to a certain point, she or he will refer you to someone who can continue working with you to enhance your spiritual growth.

And don't forget that *all-important* Sabbath rest from Friday sunset to Saturday sunset, when secular labor and focus is ceased and special attention is given to prayer, worship with fellow believers, study of God's word, service, and spending time out in nature.

CHAPTER 23

Be Thankful No Matter What

Remember to be thankful whatever your situation, because there's *always* someone who has it *worse* than you do that would *gladly* trade places with you. Serve others regularly. By nature we're selfish. However, if we regularly practice altruism (serving others, expecting nothing in return) selfishness can be purged, and selflessness will take its place. Helping others regularly also changes your perspective, *for the better,* in regards to your own self and life. You begin to think, "I don't really have it bad."

A thankful spirit comes in handy during rough academic times. You may find yourself thinking something like, "School is hard, but at least I'm in school and able to prepare for my career. There are thousands who wish they had the opportunity I have. Thank you Lord for opening this door of opportunity for me?" Helping others in need also reduces self-centeredness, and improves mood and a sense of well-being.[77,78] If your joy comes more from *giving* than getting, then you have plenty of opportunities to feel that way. Plus, joy from giving lasts much longer than joy from getting, and can be easily reinforced by continuing to give. So, no more hands out empty to receive, but full to give.

CHAPTER 24

Believe that Your Hard Work Will Be Worth it All

Believe that you *will* eventually graduate with a degree or certificate that will be worth the sacrifice. From a purely economic standpoint, those with a college degree typically make more money in the long run than those without such education. This money can be used to support the mission of your church and other worthy causes and, of course, to pay the expenses that come with life. Also, those with further formal education report greater career satisfaction and feeling better about themselves and life than do those who have been unable to attain educationally. Persevere at obtaining your education no matter how challenging it is; at the least, the degree will mean much more to you because it didn't come easy.

Should you fall short in applying the strategies in this book, which is bound to happen every now and then, don't be discouraged; get up, dust yourself off, and pray for power to press on in the Lord's strength.

Your *best* days are ahead!

APPENDIX A

(1) Stop procrastinating
(2) Exercise at least three times a week
(3) Practice my religion more seriously

How I and my life will be if I *don't* achieve these goals	How I and my life will be if I *do* achieve these goals
Stress regarding tests and assignments	Reduced stress regarding tests and assignments
Poor grades on tests and assignments	Improved academic performance
Parents on my case because of low grades	My parents will be pleased with my academic performance
Low energy	I'll have more energy throughout the day
Gaining more weight than is healthy	My weight will come down
Feel self-conscious about my appearance	I'll like better the way I look in the mirror
Worry too much	I'll worry much less
Fearful of the future	I'll trust God to take care of the future
Engage in behavior I know isn't right	I'll give in to temptation less
Low self-worth	I'll feel better about myself

References

1. Miller, L.H., & Smith, A.D. (2001). *Stress audit questionnaire* (adapted). Boston, MA: Boston Medical Center.

2. Family Heritage Books. (2001). *Radiant living.* Wildwood, GA: Family Heritage Books.

3. Anonymous. (1998). *Academic perfectionism* screening scale (adapted).

4. Anonymous. (1998). *Codependency screening scale* (adapted).

5. Ludington, A., & Diehl, H. (2002). *Health power: Health by choice, not chance.* Hagerstown, MD: Review and Herald Publishing Association.

6. Pargament, K.I. (1997). *The psychology of religion.* New York, NY: Guilford Press.

7. Lambert, L.M., Fincham, F.D., Stillman, T.F., Graham, S.M., & Beach, S.R.H. (2009). Motivating change in relationships: Can prayer increase forgiveness? *Psychological Science, 21*(1), 126-132.

8. Sondag, S. (2008, July 26). State ban on serving trans fat first in United States. *San Francisco Chronicle,* p. A-1.

9. Downs, M.F. (2008). *The truth about 7 common food additives.* WebMD. Retrieved August 7, 2008 from http://www.webmd.com/diet/features/the-truth-about-seven-common-food-additives.

10. Ludington & Diehl. (2002).

11. Family Heritage Books. (2001).

12. Craig, W.J. (1993). *Eating for good health.* Eau Claire, MI: Great Harvest Books.

13. Ludington & Diehl. (2002).

14. Craig. (1993).

15. Family Heritage Books. (2001).

16. Ibid.

17. Rainda, H. (1992). Vegetarianism, the way to go. *Health and Healing Journal, 11*(4).

18. Ingersoll, B. (1989, February 2). Meat inspection cuts proposed by Reagan. consumerists say plan to end daily checks comes just as food poisoning rises. *Wall Street Journal Midwest Edition.*

19. Shinn, A., & Mui, Y.Q. (2008, August 10). Whole foods recalls beef processed at plant long at odds with USDA. *Washington Post*, p. A01.

20. Downs. (2008).

21. Thrash, A.M., & Thrash, C.L. (1996). *Nutrition for vegetarians.* Seale, AL: NewLifestyle Books.

22. Downs. (2008).

23. Family Heritage Books. (2001).

24. Ludington & Diehl. (2002).

25. Family Heritage Books. (2001).

26. Mangels, A.R. (2003). Position of the American dietetic association and dieticians of Canada: Vegetarian diets. *Journal of the American Dietetic Association, 103* (6), 746-765.

27. Ludington & Diehl. (2002).

28. Sinha, R., Cross, A.J., Graubard, B.I., Leitzmann, M.F., & Schatzkin, A. (2009). Meat and mortality: A prospective study of over half a million people. *Archives of Internal Medicine, 169* (6), 562-571.

29. The World Cancer Research Fund/American Institute for Cancer Research. (2007). *Food, nutrition, physical activity, and the prevention of cancer: A global perspective.* Washington, D.C.: American Institute for Cancer Research.

30. Ibid.

31. Griffin, V.B, Griffin, D.J., & Hulse, V. (1997). *Move over milk: The udder side of dairy.* Hot Springs, NC: Let's Go.

32. Ibid.

33. O'Brien, M. (1998). *Alternative medicine: An objective view.* Berkeley, CA: Institute of Natural Resources.

34. Downs. (2008).

35. Ludington & Diehl. (2002).

36. Mindell, E., & Zucker, M. (June 1988). The worst food additives. *Prevention*, 111-113.

37. Ibid.

38. Ibid.

39. Ludington & Diehl. (2002).

40. Radiant Living. (2001).

41. Moore, R., & Moore, D. (1986). *Homemade health: A family guide to nutrition, exercise, stress control, and preventive medicine.* Dallas, TX: Word Publishing.

42. Mindell & Zucker. (1988).

43. Thrash & Thrash. (1996).

44. Mindell & Zucker. (1988).

45. Downs. (2008).

46. Mindell & Zucker. (1988).

47. Ibid.

48. Downs. (2008).

49. Ibid.

50. Mindell & Zucker. (1988).

51. Downs. (2008).

52. Mindell & Zucker. (1988).

53. Thrash & Thrash. (1996).

54. Radiant Living. (2001).

55. Ibid.

56. Ludington & Diehl. (2002).

57. Craig. (1993).

58. Berkman, L.F., & Breslow, L. (1983). *Health and ways of living.* New York, NY: Oxford University Press.

59. Craig, W.J. Health Ministry Class Lecture, July 2, 1997. Berrien Springs, MI: Andrews University.

60. Craig, W.J. Health Ministry Class Lecture, June 19, 1997. Berrien Springs, MI: Andrews University.

61. Ludington & Diehl. (2002).

62. Health Letter Associates. (1995). *Wellness made easy: 365 tips for better health.* Berkeley, CA: School of Public Health, University of California at Berkeley.

63. Chakravarty, E.F., Hubert, H.B., Lingala, V.B., & Fries, J.F. (2008). Reduced disability and mortality among aging runners. *Archives of Internal Medicine, 168*(15), 1638-1646.

64. Radiant Living. (2001).

65. Sobel, D.S., & Ornstein, R. (1996). *The Healthy mind healthy body handbook.* New York, NY: Patient Education Media, Inc.

66. Proctor, S. Health Ministry Class Lecture, June 23, 1997. Berrien Springs, MI: Andrews University.

67. Ludington & Diehl. (2002).

68. Radiant Living. (2001).

69. Ibid.

70. O'Brien. (1988).

71. Ibid.

72. Sobel & Ornstein. (1996).

73. Ibid.

74. Ludington & Diehl. (2002).

75. American Psychological Association. (2003). Spirituality and mental health. *Monitor on Psychology, 31*(11), 40-53.

76. McCullogh, M.E. (1995). Prayer and health: Conceptual issues, research review, and research agenda. *Journal of Psychology and Theology, 23*, 15-29.

77. Radiant Living. (2001).

78. Sobel & Ornstein. (1996).

About the Author

Dr. Carlton H. Oler is a licensed psychologist and professor of psychology. He has over 30 years of clinical and teaching experience in a variety of mental health and academic settings in many parts of the United States. He has been voted by psychology majors as "Instructor of the Year," "Most Inspirational Teacher," "Most Interesting Class," and "Most Christ-like." Dr. Oler is also a Health Service Psychologist, Master Addictions Counselor, and Board Certified Professional Christian Counselor.

He is a graduate of Lowell High School (San Francisco, California); has a B.A. in Psychology from San Francisco State University; an M.S. in Counseling and Mental Health from California State University, East Bay; and a Ph.D. in Clinical Psychology from the University of Cincinnati. Dr. Oler completed a predoctoral fellowship in the Department of Psychiatry at Yale University School of Medicine and a postdoctoral residency in the Psychiatry Department at Kaiser Permanente Medical Center (Oakland, California).

He has also taken coursework in the Master of Divinity Program at Andrews University Theological Seminary, and served as an associate pastor. Dr. Oler has published articles in journals such as *Psychotherapy, Social Work*, and *Social and Behavioral Sciences*. He is also an avid reader of anything related to health, and has conducted or co-conducted hundreds of mental health, relationship health, physical health, and spiritual health seminars nationally and internationally.

Dr. Oler has taught and counseled students from high school to graduate school. He desires to see all students achieve optimum health mentally, relationally, physically, and spiritually as well as reach their fullest academic potential and satisfaction.

For recreation, Dr. Oler enjoys time with his family, 5K racing, playing Scrabble, and keeping up with the latest holistic health advances.

Made in the USA
Middletown, DE
04 April 2016